From Grief into

VISION

ל

OTHER WORKS BY DEENA METZGER:

FICTION:

Skin: Shadows/Silence
The Woman Who Slept With Men to Take the War Out of Them
What Dinah Thought
The Other Hand
Doors: A Fiction for Jazz Horn

NON-FICTION:

Writing for Your Life: A Guide and Companion to the Inner Worlds
Tree: Essays and Pieces
Intimate Nature: The Bond Between Women and Animals
(with Brenda Peterson and Linda Hogan)
Entering the Ghost River:
Meditations on the Theory and Practice of Healing
Sacred Illness/Sacred Medicine
(with Michael Ortiz Hill)

POETRY:

Dark Milk
The Axis Mundi Poems
Looking for the Faces of God
A Sabbath Among the Ruins

PLAYS:

The Book of Hags
Not As Sleepwalkers
Dreams Against The State

AUDIO:

This Body/My Life

From Grief into VISION

A Council

ל

DEENA METZGER

HAND TO HAND

From Grief Into Vision: A Council is sponsored by Mandlovu, a nonprofit educational member organization of International Humanities Center (IHC). Mandlovu was created to support visionary artists, writers, and healers who are committed to the exploration, revitalization, and preservation of indigenous wisdom and medicine traditions as paths to planetary healing and peacemaking on behalf of all beings. Because of the global challenge of these most difficult times, Mandlovu's goal is to sustain those teachers and practitioners whose work is devoted to the generation and manifestation of new forms of consciousness.

We are very grateful to the AnJel Fund of RSF Social Finance for their most generous support.

Book produced and designed by Stephan David Hewitt.

Front cover image: "The Ambassador" by Stephan David Hewitt, from an original photo by Cynthia Travis. Back cover image photo by Deena Metzger. Photos of Deena on author page and back cover by Ayelet Berman-Cohen.

ISBN 978-0-9720718-0-2

Manufactured in the USA by Hand to Hand, P.O. Box 186, Topanga, CA, 90290.

Contents

ACKNOWLEDGEMENTS

This book is a Council. It has come to be through many different voices conversing and meditating with each other. We were called together through our common grief but once we were gathered, possibility revealed itself. The voices in this book are not all human voices; this is why there is possibility even in these times.

And so I gratefully acknowledge and thank everyone who has become a part of this book: from the most devoted editor and publisher Stephan David Hewitt, and the Elephant Ambassador, the Speaker for the Wild, to the human voices of healing, peacebuilding and community as well as the spirits and ancestors who have come forth on behalf of restoration of the natural world and divine beauty. As you read the voices recorded in this work, you will understand and share with me the deep gratitude that I feel for the partnership, camaraderie and vision that could only emerge from among us. Here also I acknowledge the luminous web that is Daré and beyond Daré, allies, friends and kin, the community of souls committed to the future, whom I have had the privilege to know.

I particularly want to express my deep gratitude to Cynthia Travis and to Krystyna Jurzykowski whose spiritual companionship and most generous support have sustained me in so many ways in my life and also while thinking about and writing this work. Similarly, I gratefully acknowledge Michele Daniels, Suzanne Marks and Susan Jackson who have heard the call to offer such work to the world and have most kindly responded. These friends and companions have helped vision become manifest. I, we, could not have done this without them.

Here, also, gratefulness to my most dear ones, my sons Greg and Marc, and my husband, Michael Ortiz Hill, for in such love and connection lies the future.

And to you the reader, I thank you for considering these words and hope that you will join with us in your own wise and luminous ways to assure a future for all beings.

In Gratitude:

Joanna Macy's pioneer work, *The Council of All Beings*, The Nuclear Guardianship Project and her recognition of the existence of future beings, foremothered this work. Thankfully, she continues to lead us toward possibility.

At the Threshold of the Unknowable...

In Homage to *Hopscotch* and Julio Cortázar

TABLE OF INSTRUCTIONS

In its own way, this book consists of many essays, but two above all.

The first can be read in a normal fashion from beginning to end, without being distracted by the inserts, footnotes, commentaries, links to other websites, addenda and references.

In this manner, the reader may ignore what follows with a clear conscience.

The second can be read, beginning at the beginning, and following the sequence indicated by the inserts and internal references and links.

An infinite number of other essay possibilities occur through encouraging the reader to follow now this insert or link and now that insert and link to wherever they lead, returning directly to the text, or stopping to meditate, journey, contemplate, or write oneself, going where one is called in whatever form intrigues or informs the mind and spirit of the reader. Imagine the book, originally conceived as a website linking to other websites, that it may well become in the future, as an engaging conversation between peers, a council that necessarily includes the readers and encourages us to weave our stories into the mix. As a pdf file is be available on the website **www.deenametzger.com**, it could be useful to open one's own file for response that can later be included in the reader's version of the text, or use the blank spaces and pages provided to enter into the dialogue that the author hopes will engage the reader. Email and web addresses are provided when possible so that the conversation can include all those who are participating in imagining viable futures for all beings.

*A*lready I felt overwhelmed by history, a despair for wild beauty, and a suspicion that all was lost.

– Christopher Shaw, *Sacred Monkey River* [i]

$\mathcal{I}$ have wanted to write this since I returned in October from the pilgrimage to Botswana to meet with the Elephant Ambassadors and to Liberia with **everyday gandhis** to participate in their visionary peace-building efforts in West Africa.

But first, you must understand that the Elephant Ambassadors came yet again.

Nothing that will be written here must undermine, or detract from, the incomprehensible, but incontrovertible occurrence – the Elephant Ambassador that came to several of us in Botswana in 2000 and again in 2001 came again, this time with his community to meet our community, in September 2005. Trying to understand and respond to this miraculous event is an integral part of responding to the environmental and political crises that threaten the continuing existence of the planet because it urgently requires, like so many other similar incidents that we have all experienced, a thoughtful and heartfelt reassessment of the true nature of reality and the consequences and possibilities of the ways we live our lives.

❧

If the spirits and the Divine are real then this world we humans have created has become a sacrilege.

❧

In the world, as western mind has defined it, it is hard to return to the ways of the spirits and to be open to them, to acknowledge them and to yield to them publicly. Nevertheless, there are too many events and occurrences, like the advent of the Elephant Ambassadors, that cannot be explained logically but can be understood by recognizing multiple and diverse intelligences, and the activity, guidance and intervention of Spirit, the Divine and its many faces.

❧

"… Take an axe to the cherry orchard. How the trees are going to fall. We're going to build new houses and our grandchildren and all our descendants are going to know a new life in this land."

Stage right, we hear the sound of the axe.

–Anton Chekhov, *The Cherry Orchard*

These words marking the end of an insufferable elite also marked the beginning of the end of the land. The new life became the Soviet Union and Stalin and everything that followed from state terror to the gulags to Chernobyl.

In trying to understand or come closer to the true nature of reality, compromised by the narrow parameters imposed by Western thought, many thoughtful people informed by wisdom from different cultures, indigenous understanding and their own experience, recognize dreaming as an essential way of knowledge. People who have access to this stream of knowing are "dreamers". Lawrie Hartt is a dreamer. This voice and commentary is from an email exchange between us. "On my return home to Philadelphia after the retreat to Santa Cruz Island with members of the Daré community and also Shona *Nganga* (medicine man) Mandaza Kandemwa, I'd settled into a book during the flight when I noticed above me on the video monitor one scene after another of falling trees. Down they came, whole forests full. The video playing on the airline for all to see was the history of the chainsaw. That night I dreamed a funeral for trees."

Lawrie's dream of the funeral for trees reminds me of the dream I had election day, 11/01/04:

Expecting the septic people, I look out the window and see a huge tree, cut down lying on a flat bed truck, as if its roots were flailing. I realize that all the trees, all the trees on our property have been cut down. All the trees are cut down and can't be rescued.

George Washington also felled a cherry tree. (A little humor here, perhaps, through the comparison with Chekhov). Still the settlers of the "New World" did cut down the forests. The heirs of those settlers continue to raze the world. From the proliferation of depleted uranium [§], toxic chemicals and defoliants to our gulags at Guantanamo, Abu Ghraib and hidden away elsewhere, our inner and outer, physical and spiritual landscapes have been almost entirely devastated.

Cutting down the trees, we are cutting down the World Tree, the *axis mundi*, the very world itself.

೧೨

There is a strong possibility that the Mayan civilization failed before the Spanish invaded because they cut down the trees and this led to drought conditions. As a consequence, the custom may have developed that continues today of doing ceremony, making offerings and asking forgiveness of nature for killing one of its creations when clearing land for planting or cutting a tree for a house.

The growing Mayan population gradually began to consume ever-greater amounts of their most crucial resource, wood. Just as our own society is vitally dependent on petroleum, the world of the Classic Maya depended on the consumption of trees. Besides wood's use for bathing, preparing corn, and the building of homes, it was required to make lime, the crucial ingredient in the mortar and stucco needed in the creation of Mayan architectural monuments. The increasingly widespread removal of the cloud-producing forest cover in the Mayan lowlands eventually led to prolonged periods of drought in the region and increasing warfare between competing alliances of cities.

– Robert Sitler, from an unpublished manuscript, The Mayan Road [ii]
See also: http://www.stetson.edu/~rsitler

[§] *See BBC News article: Depleted Uranium: The Next Generation, http://news.bbc.co.uk/1/hi/sci/tech/1122566.stm (among so many other articles) as to the toxic effects of the usage of DU.*

My writing life, at three, began with a poem of a tree growing in a child's hand. And now, the axes are everywhere.

❦

"Tree" is what I called the poster I brought into the world of a woman, myself, with her chest tattooed after a mastectomy, her arms raised to the sky, after the book I had written about the way of healing from cancer. But the public named it the Warrior poster; the name stuck. The tree, a symbol of life, was renamed for war, inevitably an act against the tree itself.

Many people, particularly those of dominating cultures, reserve certain qualities for themselves and call them human. Observation reveals, however, that many of these qualities, like compassion and empathy, are shared by animals and even plants.

Reading *The Field*, by Lynn McTaggert, I am compelled to understand a familiar experiment in an entirely different way:

A plant's leaves are burned. The plant exhibits the signs of pain. Another plant's leaves are burned. The first plant, still hooked up to a monitor, exhibits signs of pain.

Compassion? The world is a field of compassion, I think. What are the implications of such an insight? How the plants and animals and stones and bacteria must be suffering each day as a consequence of those of our activities that are enacted against them. They suffer their own pain and everything's pain. All of it. I am taken by the joy of understanding this, of the truth of this possibility and the anguish of it. When I return to *The Field*, I read, "This suggested that the plant had received this information via some extrasensory mechanism and was demonstrating empathy. It seemed to point to some sort of interconnectedness between living things. ... As in *Star Wars*, each death was registered as a disturbance in the field."

I have to close the book to give homage to the moment. Each death is registered.... Each death is registered....

I sink into the implications ... I feel the deaths ... each death is being registered ... in this moment. Now.

— *From an unpublished letter from Deena Metzger to Joanna Macy, March 2005.*

Consciousness at this time requires us to revision the nature of trees and understand not only our relationship to them but that they are indeed our relations.

> Now the forest was gone. It had vanished so fast, was still vanishing, that people my own age had a hard time internalizing the new reality. And the Chol people in the vicinity [of Palenque] when you saw them along the road or disappearing into the undergrowth with machetes in hand wore a look I came to associate with the landscape's radical transformation. It was the same look of stunned disbelief that you saw in photographs of the survivors of bombings, urban renewal, and other ravages–their fields salted, their wells poisoned, the world reconfigured in the blink of an eye.

— Christopher Shaw, *Sacred Monkey River: A Canoe Trip with the Gods*[iii]

Chris Shaw is associated with **Ríos Mayas**, a loose affiliation of independent conservationists, archaeologists, scientists, writers, artists and citizens in Mexico, Guatemala, and the United States, dedicated to the preservation of free-flowing rivers and watershed management in the Maya region of Mesoamerica. "We propose geographic and biological continuity, archaeological preservation, low-impact tourism, and equal rights and economic opportunity for local populations as our primary objectives. These forces are necessary to achieve a collective sense of place, a corresponding sense of possibility, peaceful change, and appropriate development in the region. http://www.gomaya.com/riosmayas/ or email: risomayas@gomaya.com. *(See endnote i)*

At times in our lives, my husband, Michael Ortiz Hill, and I have played a game of beauty. Out on the land, we would gather small stones and begin to order them into tiny worlds, niches, labyrinths, spirals and circles, centers and perimeters, creatures, inhabitants, beings in exact and unexpected relationship to each other. Each of us, moving in turn, tried to find the coherence that is the realm of beauty. Each gesture modified the original conception and required the other to meet the emerging configuration that could not, ever, be predicted. Sometimes a twig, a blossom or a seed through the exquisite rightness of its placement so exactly and unexpectedly completed the work that we thought we had glimpsed the mystery of creation, while other times inattention, an awkward gesture, the mere brush of a sleeve, impatience, irritation, brought everything tumbling down, one stone toppling another, until utter disorder, chaos, inalterable destruction followed.

After reading about James Lovelock's new work, *The Revenge of Gaia*, February 2006, pronouncing the imminent extinction of everything, I dreamed a world of *chaos*, but only when I couldn't find enough coherence in the dream to recognize the story I was in, did I think we were entirely lost.

What follows is also from the long letter I wrote to Joanna Macy in March 2005. She, herself, has put much thought into our relationship with the future, with future beings and how, perhaps they may guide us. Implicit in her work are the ethics, which consider the right of future beings to their lives and the necessity upon us to act accordingly. These paragraphs are excerpted from that letter.

This letter began to imagine itself on the equinox which Michael and I spent in Joshua Tree witnessing the unprecedented outburst of wildflowers that are a glorious consequence of the unceasing rains — the consequence of global warming, the descent upon us of the melting ice caps, the release of the old ones from the chosen crystalline form they had inhabited for centuries. Beauty abounding that is not unlike the terrifying opulence of vegetation that followed the dropping of the atom bombs on Hiroshima and Nagasaki. (This beauty co-existent with horrific drought in Africa and parts of the Amazon reduced to a trickle in the summer of 2005).

I speak about the rain or the water, the elementals as beings; this is a new way of speaking or seeing that has taken me in the last years. It is a metaphor or it is a truth; I/we have no way of knowing which it is. But as I sit here in this the last week of my bi-annual attempt to descend into silence and the creative heart, I feel these spirits calling to me from somewhere in a field that isn't defined by differentiating present or future or past while recognizing that we humans do live within such a continuum and our consequent behavior affects the field within which these spirits exist. Or, perhaps there is no difference between the spirits and the field, but we cannot know this; we are outside of it.

I write this trying to extricate myself, if only for this moment, from the narrowness of my own intrinsic and inescapable limitation, the physical, mental, spiritual nature of a human being whose

senses only recognize and respond instinctively to four palpable dimensions. If there are twenty-two dimensions or no specific dimensions altogether, I can only think about them without knowing
them as my reality. Still ... these spirits ... and this moment ... and
the challenge and necessity to see that the world we are living in
is not the world but a very partial view and, therefore, an illusion.
This world as we design it is a false and dangerous construction for
beings who can invent technologies that operate according to the
laws of dimensions beyond them but without the wisdom, the ethical structures and restraints that are implicit in those dimensions.

A series of questions insert themselves here. Questions that I
have been asking myself and others when I am/we are trying to understand experiences, extra-ordinary events, for example, that
challenge our basic assumptions and everything we have been
taught. What is the true nature of the reality in which such things
happen? How are we to live according to the nature of the incomprehensible but undeniable reality that is in a multitude of forms
continuously presenting itself to us? What changes are demanded
by the world we begin to perceive?

I have trusted that the time would come that I would have assimi-
lated enough of both the awesome and the horrific events of this time
and of the last six months of my life to be able to write this.

My first commitment is to write about the elephants, the Ambassadors, the "Speakers For the Wild" who have come to us again. I say
us because they are crossing the species barrier to make themselves
known, not only to individuals, but to our communities and then to the
world. Our last meeting in September 2005 remains even now entirely
inexplicable and yet undeniable in its splendor.

"Why did the elephants come?" asked a friend and colleague, who
has been visited by whales.

"To prevent apocalypse," I answered.

She was dissatisfied with my answer. It made her extremely uncomfortable. We wrestled with the language. I argued for these words
without knowing why until now: it is to communicate the extremity of
our state and that we are responsible for it.

Finally, we agreed on another way of speaking of it:

"Why did the elephants come?"

"To restore creation."

While I was writing this essay, I sent it out to several colleagues who are part of the matrix. My hope was that they would send, for inclusion, some of those dreams, stories, experiences upon which this work is based. One of these colleagues, Nancy Myers of SEHN (Social and Environmental Health Network http://www.sehn.org/pre-caution.html) sent a long response that is excerpted below. She opened it with the paragraph about apocalypse and restoring creation.

In truth the friend whose conversation with me is recorded in that paragraph was made more than uncomfortable by my words. She actually said that she was gripped by nausea and overwhelm. I didn't understand her response as we looked for other words, as we recognized that embedded in language are perspectives, world-views, cosmologies and epistemologies and, accordingly, consequences. But when this second friend and colleague had the same visceral response to the essay, I knew I had to think hard and long about it. Michael and I had a long conversation and he said the following: "We live in a dreadful time and it does not serve us to make it less than it is. Nevertheless, this is an essay about possibility."

Taking both of my friend's responses to heart, I understood that the difference between their responses and mine might well have to do with our religious background and upbringing. I wrote:

"What I understand this morning is the difference between someone who was raised with thoughts of apocalypse and someone who was not. It is most possible that being raised Jewish, and having gone through years of soul searching to step out of western mind as best as I have been able to, I do not have the response that the friend had to my statement 'To prevent apocalypse' and the conversation that ensued .... Now that you have written, I, fortunately, understand something I didn't before ... or rather I am aware of not understanding or feeling it in the same way. And so I have to be careful but don't really know the territory because I wasn't raised there and don't live there. I am also aware that my response, or lack, is the minority response. The word or thought — apocalypse — was not in my mind until I was an adult, despite my horror of the Bomb. Hell, in the literal theological sense, was never and still is not anywhere in my thoughts.

"I had not been raised with concern about apocalypse though I do remember the yellow front cover of Junior Scholastic with the di-agram of an atom on it and an article within about the atom bomb. It was the fall of 1945. I was nine years old. I knew then that the world as I knew it or expected it to be was over and we were gravely endangered in ways that were beyond what I was already beginning to learn about the Holocaust."

I believe that the situation we are facing is as extreme as any that any people have faced since the beginning of time. And also I understand that we must find ways to speak about it that do not undermine our ability to act with heart, consciousness and hope. Radical Hope is a term I have used. Daré member Raphael Renteria has countered with Radical Commitment. Michael has chimed in with Radical Possibility.

I am certain that Nancy Myers, the writer of the letter that follows, a profound woman, writer and environmental thinker and activist, is not in denial of how grave things are but is looking for ways to speak about it that will further empower her and her community. (We have had several conversations about the level of despair and demoralization that occurs among environmentalists who receive first hand on a daily basis the horrific news of the deterioration of the environment. Therefore, I am reprinting some of what she wrote.) This is an issue we must all wrestle with, recognizing that each of us will write differently, respond differently, until a full and effective council is achieved. A council does not mean that all voices are equally represented in the self-serving manner that the media pretends to give equal time to all opinions. We are looking here for all the perspectives and understandings that gather to receive counsel from each other, the voices that are intrinsic to the work of restoring creation with the realization that they create a harmonic that is not just an aggregate of oppositions. Here is what she wrote:

"I am sending this with trepidation ....The metaphor that most accurately applies to my response to your essay is allergy. I had an allergic response. It caused my spirit to swell up and shut down and made it hard for me to breathe. I don't have any good ideas or alternatives but, understand, this apocalypse talk and the chaotic urgency of your essay began... to feel as coercive as evangelistic hellfire sermons used to feel to me as a 6-year-old. I 'came to Jesus' many times under such pressure because it scared the hell out of me. The altar call was always called an 'invitation.' But there was nothing invitational about it. It was sheer, fear-based pressure.... Later I saw it as violent, violating, coercive, and I understood how, because of the extreme vision of potential damnation, kind and good people became coercive.

"Now I can say they were just wrong. Their vision of apocalypse is not mine. There are other, genuine, human-made apocalypses to fear and I do share your understanding of that. And yet I am trying to make sense of my allergic reaction to it, which is more than just childhood conditioning. Apocalypse talk was a strident stream in the culture around the Bulletin of the Atomic Scientists. The extreme nature of nuclear power stirred it up, often in the good/evil dichotomy: infinite power for good or evil (well now we know it's all bad of course). And the only way to get people to pay attention is to scare them, show them the horror. Ultimately, I came to sense that stirring the fear, showing the horror, real as it was, was an incomplete response, as incomplete as the politics/policy one, as incomplete as relying on human intelligence. Maybe it moved some people but it would never move me except to turn away. It felt dead, like death. Ultimately it drained me dry and I had to move away from the whole issue."

When I received this letter, I wrote back to say among other things. "I do not intend this book to be a sandwich board and I hope it does not sound like I am walking down the street yelling, "The world is coming to an end! Repent!" Nevertheless, it is not hysteria for the purpose of conversion that causes me to remind us that the times are grave; extinction is possible. It is necessary for us to change our lives, to find the paths that can avert this unspeakable catastrophe for all life.

On the issue of apocalypse, Michael Ortiz Hill says: "Beware the seduction of the image, mine and others, for the myth of apocalypse seeks to enthrall us into an epic fiction with very real consequences. Beware the fascination with what is larger than life, this vulgar Passion Play that would crucify the world."[iv]

Ironically, Michael's caution came out of wrestling with me about these same questions in 1988:

"In my original draft of the ritual, I succumbed to the temptation of answering the pathos of apocalypse with an apocalyptic gesture — I planned a ritual act of burning the scriptures of apocalypse (the tenth chapter of the *Bhagavad-Gita* and the end of the Book of Revelation) at Ground Zero. My wife rather sensibly suggested that, instead of trying to meet the Manhattan Project by replicating its grandiosity, perhaps tenderness and humility might bear the proper attitude of healing in such a dark period of history."[v]

And in another context, I wrote the following to Stephen Karcher. a contemporary translator and interpreter of the I Ching. He has had the foresight to include the original shamanic pre-Confucian understandings in his book *Total I Ching: Myths for Change*; the original texts were not patriarchal, and truly describe the nature of change.

Dear dear Stephen:

The way the oracle speaks so directly is terrifying. I just read the attached and another article about Lovelock that was just published today preceding the pub date of his new book *The Revenge of Gaia*. Essentially, he says, it is all over. And so I thought, Ok, it is all over. We have all received a death sentence. How then do we proceed? How do we live our lives when there isn't any hope of posterity? What does Spirit intend? Hope for? Is there a chance? In answer to my question, I got 38 Diverging/The Shadow Lands:

(It is all things outside: isolation, danger, foreigners, wilderness, punishments, the Demon Country. It suggests strange visions, alternate realities and chance meetings with important spirit beings... This is the world of the *wugui*, the shamans or intermediaries who deal with angry ghosts and spirit presence outside the normal and of the border regions, beyond the frontiers ... Dealing with these spirits, transforming the negative power of the ghost world into a creative tension with the living is essential to the continuation of human life and culture. This is the job of the wandering sage, the one who voyages outside the norms, the *wugui*.)

Well, you could have guessed, couldn't you? No changing lines. Perfect. A real answer. Then I asked about a novel I am writing. I mean if Lovelock is even close to right, why write a novel? The answer was 60, Articulating the Crossings:

(The root is bamboo: nodes or joints on the plant, the strips of bamboo used for books, a bamboo flute and its natural measures or intervals. It is a chapter, a paragraph, an interval, a key or significant detail, a tablet attesting a mandate, the annual or seasonal feasts and rituals that articulate a sacred time. ...Express your thought. ...Make chapters, sections and units of time ... Articulating is pleasing to the spirits. By using "Articulating" to shape the measures and the times, property will not be injured and the people will not be harmed.)

Articulating the Crossings was also the hexagram that I received when we sat together to seek advice regarding 9/11. *Entering the Ghost River* was, ultimately, my response to the divination.

To this, Stephen Karcher answered:

"I read Lovelock (it is circulating) and to me the top line of your reading about writing covers it well: 60.6 no bitter articulating. Whatever he might be as a Planet Doctor, this piece freezes people in fright, as it froze you. Let's not do that. Let's articulate what we have to articulate quietly and joyously (60.4) and take our job of being Shamans of the Shadow seriously in that spirit. Remember, the basic lesson of Change is that the future is a Gamble with the Gods, a place where we can help change the flow of things in the heart. I have become allergic to apocalyptic visions of all sorts."

Having brought these voices together, I place before us the dilemma that the threat of apocalypse has been in the imagination for a long time and has distorted the lives of billions. However, this time, in fact, the situation is graver than we have ever imagined. If we are undermined in our activity and hope, by the reference to apocalypse, it may be necessary to find other ways to face our circumstances without projecting that trope and further undermining our situation. My understanding of apocalypse implies total devastation; it has no hint in it of divine or Godly intent or connection. Rather, it is the opposite, total devastation enacted against the earth by human beings. It is essential to leave God out of apocalypse as we are seeking to save creation and some of us understand creation as an ongoing divine energy and event. What then shall we say? How can we call each other to bear witness to what is occurring and do everything we can, devote our entire lives to the restoration of the natural world?

It was Lovelock's analysis that goes far beyond a warning that led me to use the word apocalypse. In council at the Topanga Daré, in an effort to stand together before what we must face as members of the human community, we consider the ways in which we live in denial of our real circumstances. Is our failure to have a word to describe the possible total destruction of the environment and all its creatures a sign of the extent of our denial of our current circumstances and the ways in which we have brought them about?

At Daré we face our denial in part in response to an essay that Daré member, Raphael Renteria, is circulating:

> People will never spontaneously take action themselves unless they receive social support and the validation of others. Governments in turn will continue to procrastinate until sufficient numbers of people demand a response. To avert further climate change will require a degree of social consensus and collective determination normally only seen in war time, and that will require mobilisation across all classes and sectors of society.

Anyone concerned about this issue faces a unique historical opportunity to break the cycle of denial, and join the handful of people who have already decided to stop being passive bystanders. The last century was marked by self-deception and mass denial.

There is no need for the 21st Century to follow suit.

–from "The Psychology of Denial: Our Failure to Act Against Climate Change"
by George Marshall[vi]

In a classic example of denial, Paul Krugman quotes James Inhofe, the chairman of the Senate Committee on Environment and Public Works as declaring: "man-made global warming is possibly the greatest hoax ever perpetrated on the American people." (*New York Times*, May 8, 2006)

ଔ

What I am concerned with here is the state of the earth, ways of meeting the crisis, the real lives of all the living beings, the possible sentience of the elementals, the ways in which spiritual practices and oracles, assistance beyond the human, might assist us in meeting this time.

On the Sentience of the Elementals

Water Speaks to the People of the World (02/18/05)

This morning I awaken to heavy rain. A short distance below my house, a landslide threatens the only road and the small house perched above it. Some miles away at the entrance to Topanga Canyon, where floods and firestorms have become familiar occurrences, a huge boulder the size of a multistory house descended in the last rains. Perhaps it was dislodged because earlier fires had destroyed the root system that held it in its place on the mountain or because the cycle of man-made drought and flood has undermined the land. As I write these words, I am praying that Water will speak through me in this critical time; the rain increases as if to confirm the remarkable possibility that the Elementals may speak to us. In the past, the water spirits have spoken eloquently to those who were faithful to them. Might it happen again? I wouldn't normally think to write these words. But it seems that we are equally confronting devastation and the Mystery. Which path we take will determine the fate of the world and of creation.

For millennia, traditional societies have recognized and honored the deities — Water, Fire, Earth and Air; these same societies have lived in dynamic and harmonic relationship with the planet. The contemporary world culture that disdains such beliefs as primitive or heathen has enacted a holocaust upon the environment equal to the worst periods of climactic change and extinction. In traditional societies one approaches the water deities or water spirits with reverence, knowing they nourish and purify all things. Now, the water is itself defiled. If the water is defiled, how can we heal the water?

At the zoo, I encounter a young father who has Mayan glyphs on his arms. "I am of the Mayan-Aztec tradition," he says. "One glyph is the dragon-water snake representing purification; the other glyph represents the bones of the ancestors. Before we enter a conflict, we purify ourselves in a sweat lodge," he says. "Then, we ask the ancestors to guide us."

My colleague, Carol Sheppard, dreams a pterodactyl, First Bird, who flies with her over the cities of the world so that she can see the autos, machines and chimneys belching black smoke into the atmosphere. "You are defiling the bones of the old ones, the ancestors," the pterodactyl berates her. Carol awakens knowing there are will be consequences of our sacrilege. *(See page 90 for full text of the dream.)*

Donna Augustine Thunderbird Turtle Woman patiently disinters the improperly buried bones of her Migmag ancestors, prepares the graves in the sacred manner, cleans the bones, wraps them and reburies them with the right prayers. Keeping a weeklong vigil in the snow and rain, she is nevertheless restored herself, her soul eased, her heart lightened. Restoring the old ways, entering into the rituals of respect and purification, honoring the ancestors and accepting their guidance, changes our relationship to the earth and revives people emotionally and spiritually.

If, over centuries, we have asked water to purify us, may we also attempt now, the sacred obligation of reciprocation? How do we meet the divine that we have defiled? Can we purify the water?

I was standing before the Ocean with environmentalist, Carolyn Raffensperger, also of SEHN (Social and Environmental Health Network http://www.sehn.org/precaution.html) who has been actively writing the Precautionary Principle into national and international law. She had been speaking of the crippling despair of environmentalists who must be aware of each detail of the process of devastation, and of her anguish before the young students who ask her why they should not hasten apocalypse so that the world can be rid of the human element quickly enough for the natural world to restore itself. It is as if they are considering being suicide bombers in a jihad on behalf of the environment.

She pauses. The sun is about to set. She says, "You know, there is only one ocean. We give the waters many different names, differentiating one area from another, but there is only one ocean." As she speaks, I am aware of the ocean that is inside me as well as the ocean I am standing before. I can no more distinguish the waters within me from the Pacific without than I can the Pacific from the Sea of Japan or the Coral Sea. I understand we are one being. And then I hear her say what I have also thought so many times that her words resound like a chorus sung, perhaps by the gulls who just hovered in the air around us as we threw bread into the wind, so many winged angels receiving our offerings and prayers, "Any act against the environment, is an act against God."

At this moment, the sky and ocean are radiant as the light of the setting sun expands orange and amber and catches on the spray and the waves, spilling golden and pooling iridescent at the edge of the surge as it hits the beach. In the Hebrew tradition, the word *esh*, fire, and *mayim*, water, combine to form *sh'mayim*, heaven. So I assume that the Presence is revealing itself to us and we must be humbly attentive.

The light fades as quickly as it emerged and we make our way back along the beach. A small bird is seated on the sand as if on a nest and watches us intently but without moving at all and yet meeting us eye to eye; its gaze is intentional. We slow down, move respectfully away so as not to cause it any trepidation. Finally, we stop altogether and watch. It stands up and turns toward the sea. Walks. Falls flat on its face. It is awful to watch this. Gets up. Falls flat. Then gets up again. It is rare to see sick birds. Finally, it makes its way to the surf and enters the sea where it seems comfortable. We do not speak. We are both wondering what we can do and are praying for its health though we do not know what has afflicted it. "May this grebe thrive."

Hours later, I read that a mysterious weeklong oil leak, due possibly to the torrential rains uncapping oil wells, has damaged more wildlife than any spill in state coastal waters since 1990 when a tanker spilled its contents.

The next day I find myself driving in rains so fierce, I cannot see the road ahead of me. It has been only eight months since I dreamed a fire coming over the ridge near my house.

In that dream, a friend, Garner MacAleer, rushes for his djembe and begins drumming in welcome the way we would in Zimbabwe if a spirit had entered the Daré hut during an *ngoma* ceremony. The meaning I gather from the dream is that Fire is a deity. The elementals are deities. This is not rhetorical.

Later that June, I drove through three forest fires raging in the vicinity of Los Angeles. Recognizing the divine in the fire, I asked Fire: What do you want? How shall we meet you? How shall we serve you?

Now, almost blinded by the crush of water, I ask the rain: What do you want? How shall we meet you? How shall we serve you?

I do not expect an answer, and yet there are unexpected words in my mind that seem to explain that this brutal rain is the release of the old water, the ancestors that have been preserved for thousands of years in the pristine glaciers, another form of living crystals whose quality, intent and intelligence is not understood by contemporary humans who observe them as dead phenomena. As in Carol Sheppard's dream, the old ones are returning, seeking a reckoning: "You will not contain us. You will not control us. You will not destroy us. You will not use us. You will not dominate us. We are autonomous and beyond you."

The old adage: Oil and water do not mix. The oil spills. The grebe is a messenger, as was the Mayan-Aztec man with glyphs on his arms representing the dragon snake, the old one, the water for purification not contamination, and the bones of the ancestors, pristine and honored. Cynical corporate aggressors cheer the melting of the northern seas so they can drill for oil where polar ice had once made the area inviolable. There will be further consequences. No one and no thing is spared in the activity of healing and realignment. The glaciers and ice caps are melting and as we cannot protect the polar bears, arctic birds and other creatures, as we cannot spare the grebes, as we cannot spare the rain, the water itself, from the consequences of our activities, we can be sure we, also, will not be spared either.

Still driving in the downpour, I know it was not right to pray for my own safety, I can only pray for the rain.

No one and no thing is spared in the great extinctions. When the smoke covers the sun, no one and no thing escapes the consequences of the lessening of the light and the intensification of the heat and the subsequent loosening of the great waters. Even as the shadow obscures the sun, the heat increases, the droughts increase, as do the floodwaters. Tsunamis batter us as great winds whirl about the globe in what, in many languages, is likened to fury. The rains pummel the mountains, the earth slides, trees are uprooted and tumble down among the boulders even as the vegetation multiplies in time to feed firestorms, which will come as surely as the rain.

The rain continues as I write. The wind comes up fierce. In the Hebrew tradition, we call the wind *ruach*; it also means breath and spirit. Rabbi Jonathan OmerMan tells me that the Hebrew word for ark, *teyvah*, also means prayer. The ark, then, that will carry us across the water, forty days and forty nights — forty implying always, a measure of water sufficient for purification and also two generations, enough to have our minds changed sufficiently to enter a new way of being — is a prayer.

I pray for Fire. I pray for Water. I pray for the Air. I pray for the Earth. I pray for the old ones, the rain, and, again, I pray for Water.

May the Waters be sacred again. May we purify them as they have purified us. May the rains come again as blessings. May the bones of our ancestors be purified, buried deeply again, laid to rest.

Horror and Beauty are standing alongside each other, as are Doom and Possibility. Which of these we ally with and call into the world depends on our consciousness and willingness and ability to step forth. How shall we know how to be and what to do in such unprecedented times when every being's life on the planet is threatened, and as Lovelock asserts, without hope of remedy?

In December 2005, I spirit-journeyed to support a small group including Oakland Daré leaders, Elenna Rubin Goodman and Garner MacAleer, and Salt Spring Daré leaders, Candace Cole and Eric Field traveling to Africa on behalf of global community including community with the animals. In that journeying, the elephants came and said, "Cross the species barrier through love. Do not do anything for us. But learn what love, real love, uninhibited love of another species, might be."

After our trip, Eric wrote to us with this dream image:

"A beautiful butterfly filled my field of vision, wings spread wide. The body to the butterfly was that of a mature, young, naked black woman. Her beauty radiated light that drew my attention to the detail on her wings where there was a collage in full color of the many faces of the African people we worked and lived with on our journey: children, parents, patients, workers, traditional healers, hosts and their children. Each face, decorated in vibrant fabrics, beads and hair styles, spoke to the meaningful connections we made in loving council, in sharing food and labor as well as in the understanding of our mutual quest for well-being.

Deena, the work we are all doing is manifesting our intentions!"

A week after Eric sent this dream of the butterfly, Thurston Seaton, whom we call Uncle Ralph, attended Daré expressly, it seemed, to tell us a dream, or rather the events that led up to a dream of butterflies. He described in detail a period of several days when he noticed a plain black butterfly with a yellow margin around its wings. It seemed that it was following him, or hovering around him and finally, though feeling entirely foolish, he asked it to communicate with him. At first it seemed to brush his shoulder and then, as he had asked it, without any hope of success, to land on his hand, it did. It repeated this for several days. Long enough for him, still disbelieving, to have it photographed on his finger.

The next day, Valerie Wolf, also dreamed a butterfly and then her friend Anthea Rice was surprised by the presence of a butterfly, like the one that befriended Uncle Ralph, in her kitchen. She tried to escort it out but it resisted and landed on her heart and stayed there a long time. Finally, it landed on her hand and she carried it out but though free it stayed with her a long time before it took off.

We find that the same animals frequently come to us simultaneously as if the mind or spirit of Butterfly is searching for a response among humans and is sending out a signal indicating the possibility of alliance and collaboration. When several people in a community ruminate on the fact and possible meanings of such visitations to each other, awareness grows and possibility develops accordingly.

The night that Uncle Ralph spoke of the butterfly, I was aware of a moth following me through the rooms. At first I assumed it followed me into the bathroom because it was seeking the light, but after awhile its behavior required me to pay attention. It landed on a piece of jewelry hanging on the wall rather far from the light that normally I would expect it to focus upon. Informed by Uncle Ralph's experience I allowed myself to enter into a surprising dialogue in which my affinities for butterflies over moths were deeply questioned. When I defended myself by saying 'Moths eat clothes and food," it chastised me, "Everything eats."

Michael has an affinity with spiders that goes beyond symbology. My affinities with insects have been largely symbolic — Spider Woman or Grandmother Spider, but not spider itself. And here I was with the moth itself. There is a difference between not harming, carefully carrying spiders, wasps, bees outside, and being in relationship with them. Now I was being called into relationship.

At the end of the dialogue, moth advised me to invite Uncle Ralph and his nephew Curtis Robinson to an event in which William

Saa would speak of his journey to Liberia to rebury his murdered brother. The moth said that we needed elders to listen to the story and that Uncle Ralph is definitely an elder.

Uncle Ralph did come to the Council and brought the following poem with him. In the way that everything here is connecting to everything else, it is a poem written in the voice of the Future Beings speaking of a museum of artifacts from the destructive time, from the time of nuclear destruction, from this time, 2006.

Relics

Skulls shrink hair strings
eyes bulge empty mouths gape
jagged teeth gleam amber
Trophy man woman hangs
askew on museum display wall

Gamma beta fingers fondle buttons
choked net fries minds
graying sky blood pressure
bloats the capillary web lace
power pistons thump stress

Clock wheel grinds pygmy years
mummy unravels wrappings
zebra stripes gorge features
balding scalp fuzz bristles
mirror projects hieroglyphics

Robot duo duel laser swords
machine rage jams output
upper excavations deepen
hot-rays penetrate
anthropological shields

Skulls shrink hair drops
eyes curl empty mouths gape
jagged teeth gleam amber
Trophy human heads droop
along alien museum walls.

Thurston Seaton, 2006

Soon after September 11, 2001, I wrote the following in *Entering the Ghost River: Meditations on the Theory and Practice of Healing*:

"Two stories intersected in that moment; a story stream-ing toward destruction and a story streaming toward healing. It is this point, this intersection of stories, the cataclysm, the possibilities that is the subject of this piece. Two stories, sep-arated by geography but not by time, becoming one story or shattering into a thousand broken shards. We are all in a story, this story now. What story led us to September 11th? What story can lead us away?"[vii]

As a world and as a community and individually, we are still in the continuation of that story. But what is the nature of that story now? Are we mired in a story leading to the imminent, irredeemable destruc-tion of the natural world and all life? Are we going to follow the weari-some and most flawed story of apocalypse proffered by President Bush and his fellow fundamentalists? Or will we choose to stand by what is truly sacred and live a story that may, still, lead us away from destruc-tiveness toward creation?

These are a few of the necessary questions for our time. They are not only questions of activity, they are questions of consciousness. They require that we scrutinize every aspect of our thinking, values and be-havior at each moment so that instead of feeding ourselves, unwittingly, to the furnaces of Moloch built in our name, we live according to prin-ciples that by our activities will determine a viable future.

In January 2006, I had a dream about President Bush, whom I am, as so many of us are, hoping will heal. *While there are strangers in the house, younger people have come to make a party without informing me. I cannot intercede as several of us are down-stairs with President George Bush who is in a wheelchair though not necessarily disabled.* "As it seems obvious, that God speaks to each of us differently," I say to him, "it is required that we try to live our lives as close to what we imagine the Divine is, so that we carry the Divine in ourselves and our actions, aware of the distinct ways we are each touched."

"I don't agree," he says and proceeds to reaffirm his own bel-ligerent beliefs and solipsistic way of thinking. As he is ailing, I think this is an opportunity to reach him, but he is not at all open to anyone or anything.

The evidence that there might still be a story that we can live to save creation comes from the confluence of great mysteries, inexplicable events, omens and portents, dreams, sacred meetings and encounters, visions, unusual and unexpected discoveries, the terrifying – because so frequent – accuracy of divinations and prophecies, the development of unexpected alliances and matrices, the sudden and pointed understanding of lost histories, (the Maya civilization, for example, whose glyphic code has been deciphered in the last thirty years) and the realization that the wisdom traditions and indigenous knowledge of the past as well as the extant spiritual and shamanic expertise of many devoted to the earth, can, and are, serving us again. The great mysteries that encourage us with the possibility of survival are being revealed to the practitioners of healing, the esoteric and the magical, as well as environmental and social activists, peace builders, and scientists whose passion is serving and saving the earth and all life. We do not have time to argue epistemologies or ways of knowing. It is not a single story. It is not exclusive. There is not one way. We are being called into a dynamic complex narrative, as intricate as the ecology of the planet, informed and created by the myriad beings walking multifarious paths on behalf of creation.

This dream of Lawrie Hartt in February, 2005 is one of those that point a way and sustain us with the possibility of restoration:

I see animals and rich plant life from all over the world, a panoply of color and celebration, come to take up residence on my heart. I realize that a rainforest is living on my heart. I hear the words, "Bear me as a seal upon your heart, for love is as strong as death and many waters cannot quench love."

This is a crossroad of mind. Like Galileo's heretical whisper, "Nevertheless it moves" – asserting that the earth is not the center of the universe but moves around the sun – it challenges everything we know and believe. At this juncture, we cannot assert that the human is the only intelligence that can save us. Human intelligence alone, the rational mind, our best thinking is incapable of rescuing us from the dire consequences of our activities. But such unprecedented events, like the reunion with the Ambassador Elephants, make it clear that other beings, unable, it seems, to counter our transgressions on their own, are showing themselves able to meet us in alliance on behalf of the world.

This is not the story we expected. We believed in evolution and presumed, as a species, we would not only survive, but thrive and sur-pass. We thought the way was to disconnect from the natural world and distinguish ourselves from other creatures and the old ways that humans cultivated over millennia. Apparently, we were wrong. The consequences of our errors are grave. Extinction. Ours and everything. And still the old ways and the beings we set ourselves against are com-ing forth again to re-establish the old alliances with all their possibilities.

It is a difficult and sorrowful story that we are in. It requires every-thing of each of us who have enough love, sorrow and courage in our hearts. We have to find the pieces of this story that may yet sustain cre-ation. "Epiphany," I wrote during a weeklong vision quest in a cave in New Mexico, "occurs as the stories in the field come together into one story." We have to bring them together, find the coherence and possi-bility among all the parts. We have to find and then live the coherent story.

That true healing, restoration and peace might come through dream, alliance with spirits, council, collaboration and vision, even though so many of us are beginning to live, successfully, according to these ways in our own lives, still seems implausible. How can these means go up against a smart bomb or an atomic missile? What short of equal strength, power and destructiveness can challenge the weapons and war machines of the world? Perhaps we are being advised to step out of the mindset that has been framed by a world devoted to the tech-nology of power, alienation and death. Can we imagine that a bomb, even The Bomb, is not the final instrument of power and domination we think it is?

The world of possibility being revealed to us is not one of our own invention but coheres in a field of connections, intersecting stories and events that includes knowledge from old wisdom traditions and stories from indigenous peoples who love the earth above all things. Here Spirit is the glue; this is a real world. Even if we are not changed enough to trust this new view of reality, nevertheless, we will benefit from yield-ing to the possibilities and wonders that are before us, to the life force and its mysterious ways. We are being called to defer to what we do not understand and what is beyond us, and what we reflexively dimin-ish as mere myths and fantasies but which, when experienced, emerge as cogent ways of knowing and living. Spiritual experiences, like Gnos-ticism and shamanism, the gathering of individual visions and stories, confirm the presence of the Divine.

ℰᴈ

So many stories and occasions demand to be included in this essay. I try to think about them as separate and distinct occurrences, but I cannot. I wanted to write about each of them, simply and individually, and I am prevented from doing so. Each calls out to the other. They are not only part of a series; they are not linked by chronology alone. There is a matrix here, an ecology of knowledge being revealed through interconnecting events and circumstances. They are part of a single piece; together they hint at a coherent story revealing something of a path. Weaving these together are dreams and other communications that come from the spirit realm.

This story is not my story. Others are living parts of the story or are dreaming the relating dreams. Together we are beginning to participate in living systems that can be expressed in writing matrices. We are looking for new forms that allow the larger story to emerge from all the stories, individual and collective.

Writing The Living Matrix: Dreams, Stories And Visions For A New Culture;

A Writing Exploration With Deena Metzger And A Community Of Committed Writers (First Initiated 12/05)

This writing retreat comes out of the experience of Dare' and Daré Immersion weeks and the annual weeklong writing intensives. It comes out of the intrigue of imagining a literature that looks to a planetary future that is not a nightmare for all beings, and that incorporates the nature of council, of the circle, of the intelligence of dreams and of the multiplicity of visions and voices and the multi-dimensionality of consciousness when we are truly awake and aligned with Spirit.

The genius of Dare' Immersion, or Community as Vision and Medicine, initiates the participant through the experiences of living in a field of interlocking stories and alliances that may at first appear random but are deeply connected and dynamic. The stories unfold and become creative and healing paths, circles or spirals, individual and collaborative. There is an intrinsic vitality to these alliances on behalf of community and all beings that emerges from living dreams and visions with integrity and aligning with the core values and rituals of indigenous practices and wisdom traditions. They have an independent life of their own: Spirit seeking expression in the world through us.

This retreat is a writing matrix that gathers people into a web of dreams, stories and voices, human and non-human to find and explore new cultural forms and language aligned with Spirit for the sake of healing, community, peacemaking, the natural world, and visions for the future.

Instead of chronological progression and the current unending, inescapable focus on conflict at the core of every piece of writing, we are seeking out another focus, the resonant forms that echo the earth's ecology, the luminous complex relationships of the universe and rigorous engagement with hope and possibility. We are committed to looking for these new forms and structures that can reflect our current complex, multi-leveled, many voiced and inter-related realities so that they may, by their nature, further the cultural process of transformation. Is it possible we are even being asked to re-imagine the printed page, an obdurately linear form, into a true council?

*Carol Sheppard, Danelia Wild and Lawrie Hartt gathered on 1/12/06 at the behest of **everyday gandhis** to discuss writing matrices and their possibilities. This is an edited record of their conversation. Because their ideas were so entirely interconnected, I took the liberty of not distinguishing one speaker from another. We could say that this, then, is the wisdom of their council:*

We are in a conversation about a modern literary form that honors all participants: the maker, the viewer/reader, the material itself. We are seeking to expand the contemporary forms so they provide mechanisms for understanding what it means to be in a story in a field of stories. We are asking: What is it to create a new culture that serves the cosmos as being interrelated?

According to the old ways, the community created a common store of living stories.

But we are also aware that there is a distinction between crafting a matrix that takes a reader in a particular direction and offering a matrix in which Spirit is the guide.

A form that allows many choices — portals. Each takes the reader somewhere that is good for everyone and everything and does not shy away from difficult material. And no one is preferenced. And the center is everywhere.

There is something else to be noted here. The nature of a portal is to be a sacred invitation. There is a difference between hearing this story, say on a bus, or in a space where Spirit has been invoked.

Each of these elements is an organism: the form, the creation, the viewer/reader; each of these has the capabilities of evolving and generating. This form is not static, but is dynamic. And so when you interact with it, you are also changed.

We are being challenged to find a form that itself, by the nature of being a form, is not a form. A formless form not unlike Deena's term 'the pathless path'. The danger is that concretizing realities adhere to forms once they are created. So, what are the forms that do not require our allegiance and that are flexible enough for the material and the reader/viewer to be pulled through to somewhere else? Then the form itself is a vehicle for or of consciousness.

We are challenged to find something that can be in relationship to the council form, the ways we carry council in Daré through stories. In Daré we ask a question and that question coheres the stories.

One enters the stream by entering into any single story or can enter into the field of stories themselves. E.g. what is the nature of peacemaking? One can enter or address the question through any story. Yes, and as healing and peacemaking are the same act, they belong at the center.

At Daré we meet each month and tell the pertinent stories. What community stories develop from the stories we carry from one month to the next?

Last year, DD told a story at Daré about encountering a woman in the street slashing herself with a broken bottle. The story articulated the many ways that DD extended help, was unable to help, and failed at helping the woman who was injuring herself. That story has lingered with me as a living presence. Every time I see someone on the street, I remember the story and it shifts my way of seeing and what action I do or do not take. Story has a living presence. The genius of council is in the coherence of stories. Many of the stories lodge in our bodies and continue to affect us and the choices we make in response. In response to what we are encountering and in response to the story we are carrying.

At first, there is simply the story — as the telling of the moment of seeing the woman slashing herself. There may be the telling of such a story casually. And, finally, there is the telling of the story in a sacred context. We've all had the experience of living a story and not understanding the enormity of the story until we have told the story in council and find ourselves in the sacred context because the community has gathered and because Spirit has been invoked.

Among us, we have been aware of learning how to live the stories (multiplex, spiritually informed interactive events, incidents, experiences) given to us as ways of knowing and paths to walk. These stories move us so because they reflect the ways in which Spirit offers guidance for the sake of the future. As these stories emerge we tell them to each other so that we may all be guided by each other's experiences. A small group of people, thus, comes to know the stories. But most people do not know them.[§] If the stories were known, then even in such times, we would have hope and direction. Writing this is part of my attempt to make some of the stories as well as the process of recognizing the stories and living accordingly, known.

But even then, as rich and useful and encouraging as these stories may turn out to be, we each have to find our own path for the sake of the world. There is no single path. But there are coherences among our paths. Together they form a coherent story that we can all live. So the earth will live. This is the nature of this prayer.

[§] *Daré communities and the NGO **everyday gandhis** have been exploring potential ways and forms of writing matrices. We are interested in innovative collaborative forms that respect and preserve the individual's experience while revealing the intelligence that emerges from interaction and commonality.*

Writing this book has reminded me that I have been experimenting with matrices and cooperative forms since I began writing, that, one book after another, I have returned to the search for forms that include many different voices. *Skin:Shadows/Silence: A Love Letter in the Form of A Novel*, my first published book, was composed of two voices in the text with "commentary" from other sources in the margins. My other novels, *What Dinah Thought*, and *The Other Hand* were more concerned with voice than character and the ways that the voices of history and myth speak through us. One early exploration was *The Woman Who Slept With Men to Take the War Out of Them*, a novel that required to be written in play form in order for the voices, the variations, to be presented authentically. There, as elsewhere, I was engaged by "Story" as opposed to plot, a concern that is articulated in both *Writing For Your Life: A Guide and Companion to the Inner Worlds* and in *Entering the Ghost River: Meditations on the Theory and Practice of Healing*.

"In Her Image: Woman's Culture," an unpublished dissertation, had white pages of text and pink pages for other voices and images. The issue of voice was very important to feminist explorations of the nature and form of woman's culture and was central to the thought that originated in the Woman's Building, LA, in the 70s where I served for five years as director of the Writing Program. My quest has always been to render the composition or harmonic of the intelligence of the different original voices of the community while rigorously avoiding dogma and orthodoxy.

Jazz is the way I thought about it in *Doors: A Fiction for Jazz Horn*. In Music Daré, we assume that the unique and spontaneous voices and instruments can come together to jam with the spirits for the sake of healing an individual and, simultaneously, the community itself. Form is content. It has political, social, spiritual implications and consequences, it organizes and affects our thinking processes and relationships as much, if not more so, than content. I am hoping that different creative and literary forms will call us into living councils and compassionate vibrant communities that by their existence will provide models for what is possible for all beings.

⌘

Last July, I was called to solitude through the dreamtime by the Mamas (initiated elders) of the Kogi people from the Sierra Nevada de Santa Marta in Columbia. It was a second call from them; the first call in

1997 led directly to establishing Daré and to other major shifts in my teaching and work on behalf of the world. Heeding this call seven years later, I spent a week in a cave in New Mexico trying to fathom their message to the world[viii] and what it was asking of me and of our community.

The cave is unlike any shelter I have ever seen, a place of remarkable and unparalleled beauty that brings together the finest human craftsmanship with the extraordinary beauty of the natural world. It was an unexpected gift to be called into solitude and silence and then to find myself so wondrously contained in the body of the earth mother.

The cave is on the land of glass and ceramic artist, Shel Neymark, in Embudo, New Mexico. It was hand carved by sculptor, Ra Paulette from *ojo caliente* sandstone. It took two years, twenty hours a week to carve it out with pick, shovel, and wheelbarrow. Then the floor, stairs, bathroom and fireplace were installed. The bathtub made with tiles by Shel Neymark is itself a wonder of design. In the center of the cave, the wood floor is laid over a deep hollow in the earth to form a drum often "played" by Neymark himself, a tap dancer.

It is hard to determine whether the astonishing beauty of the surroundings intensified or eased the rigor of being in solitude and silence asking the deep question that had to be fully addressed: What is the way I am going to live the rest of my life?

In September, following that time of silence, I cancelled an engagement to be at a gathering of elders, lineage carriers and shamans, in order to write "Katrina: Our Chernobyl."

Katrina — Our Chernobyl

Hope is a state of mind, not of the world. Hope, in this deep and powerful sense, is not the same as joy that things are going well, or willingness to invest in enterprises that are obviously heading for success, but rather an ability to work for something because it is good.

Vaclav Havel

The effects of Katrina are becoming a global tragedy like that of Chernobyl, but may yet become even more tragic and far-flung. The day after Katrina passed through the Gulf States, Gov. Haley Barbour of Mississippi said slowly and with great deliberation, "This is what Hiroshima must have looked like 60 years ago."

We dropped the bomb that devastated Hiroshima and we have not ceased and desisted since. The tragedy of Katrina is no less our responsibility and the consequence of our actions. And the tragedy of the devastation to the Gulf area is no less a global matter.

The consequences of this event show beyond a doubt that we are all involved. The Gulf tragedy, like the Indian Ocean tsunami earlier, is a dire warning for the world. It occurs within a few days of the announcements that the glaciers in the Himalayas are melting, and permafrost in the peat bogs of Siberia is melting and will release methane gas in ways that rival the progression of global warming and with even more dire results. These are the tipping points. Now how do we proceed?

How do we proceed? We do not know. When wise people are confronted by situations that are beyond them, they admit their incapacity and they call councils. We must call councils. We must call the elders, wise ones, scientists, et al., the experienced ones of the world community to confer with us and each other. Wise cultures call councils especially when they are, as we are, in grave danger of escalating the damage by taking short-term methods that can produce even greater devastation, like pouring chlorine into Lake Pontchartrain when other remedies are possible. Such cultures turn to the wise, wherever they can find them, in our case, anywhere and everywhere in the world, and they ask them to enter council and to counsel each other, governments and the people.

We must do this. Obviously, the first call must go to the environmentalists. We must find faith in each other and each other's hearts. In this instance, the wisest of environmentalists, scientists and visionaries must find each other and begin to speak to each other. They do not have to sit in the same room, but they have to find each other, find some consensus on thousands of different issues, and communicate their ideas and hopes to those who must know what is to be known and who can act upon such counsel. If a call goes out to a few whom we know are crucial, wise, experienced and sane, those few will find others. They can be encouraged to speak to whomever they know who might have pertinent information and thoughts. People know people. They can begin to confer. To council with each other.

Then the information can be funneled, by so many different means, into those organizations and entities that can act on it. We must generate generous and trusted systems of intelligence that can guide the planet at this time.

We don't need a central authority or focal point at this moment. We don't have a wise, trustworthy or capable central authority at this time. So we need the wise to begin to talk to the wise and each will find his/her own avenues. Streams becoming rivers becoming an ocean of wisdom and consciousness. Underground streams as essential as visible ones.

We must ask each other to set aside, entirely, our personal hopes for our future, for our security, for our advancement. Let us all be like those who have lost everything. We are those who have lost everything. We have all lost everything. We have. There is no future unless we understand that we have lost everything and we have to begin again. No one and no system in the living world is safe at this moment.

Some of those who have lost everything in the wake of the hurricane are in virtual prisons. Those of us who are not yet in prison, we must speak and act. So many of us have been prepared for such a moment but we need to be encouraged to speak out on behalf of life itself. The earth may still be benevolent and allow us to live but only if the earth perceives that there is an international movement of compassion and wisdom coming forth.

There is certainly no time or place for paralyzing despair, anger or politics. We have to act freely and so must act outside of governments' invitations and constraints, but act in such ways that governments are informed and required to listen and consider the wisdom that comes forth. To know the causes of what happened is essential so we will know how to proceed. We cannot simply blame the tragedy on late and insufficient response. We cannot simply blame it on not having built levees or on having diverted funds to the horrible war, with its own devastating effects on the environment, that we are perpetuating in Iraq. The causes are deeper as well and systemic. Investigation of our errors is critical as is information. We cannot abide the government refusing to allow the information we need to emerge. We cannot abide 'embedded' journalists or journalists refused entrance into a besieged area in our own country. We will not know how to proceed if we don't know what the conditions really are and what they portend.

We have to look back to see how the ways we are living our lives endanger the entire planet. Information is critical. We cannot look away now. There are many responses that are required now. No one person or group can assess them all. Let us step out of the old thinking and the old forms that have brought us here. Let us set aside all personal interest, hope for personal gain and fantasies of being safe.

Common jeopardy — and as the Lakota Sioux people say, "All our Relations," Mitakye Oyasin.

Let those who can see begin to lay out some of the far-flung implications and consequences so that we respond and act carefully. We must know the possible immediate and future environmental consequences for the people, animals, land, air and water. We must know the possible economic consequences. Economic consequences have political consequences. Political, economic and environmental consequences have social and humanitarian consequences. We must know the psychological consequences and what they portend for us as people on the planet. We must face what happens to people when they are so traumatized as people are being traumatized everywhere on the globe. We need the details, the information and the overview and we need wise, experienced and cool heads. We may not learn everything we need to know now but we can, must, at least try.

If the consequences are global then the intelligence to meet them has to be global.

Let us lay out the consequences without creating panic within ourselves or in others. This is no time for panic. Working in concert can be reassuring and stabilizing. It creates hope and calm.

There are probably other ways to proceed. I do not know them. Others may and others will come to know. That is why we meet in council. Let us search out each other to imagine the opportunities we may still have for the future. Let us find all the gates that lead toward changing our ways and responding, now, differently, and in accord with the crises and our profound hopes for a future for the world.

Some weeks later, I went to Botswana to meet with the elephants who had first called me to them in 2000.

On my return to the U. S., I gave a plenary address at the annual meeting of the American Academy of Environmental Medicine on the subject of "Fear and Cancer: What They Teach Us". I thought I knew what I would speak about as I approached the conference, but then I was compelled to speak primarily about the catastrophes we are launching and the medicine that is required to meet them. During this time, I have become increasingly aware that Daré has developed from a community of people trying to bring healing to each other to a community trying to integrate new vision with old ways of knowing for the sake of healing community itself and the world. But, the process of bringing healing to the future requires bearing witness to the past and to the present. This idea had to be inserted into the talk.

ভ৯

(As I write this, I see I must go further though there is no time or space here to detail what must be said. Still, what is Daré? *(See Page 83)* Daré is a vital non-local community of beings, including the people in all our variety, the animals, the elementals, the ancestors, and the spirits or the Divine. Whoever enters Daré with a hope for community, healing, peacemaking and a willingness to be guided by Spirit, is a member of Daré. This is the way the people tell it in Africa: When people sit in council, the ancestors are sitting in council with them. In such a way, wisdom is transferred to the community through the council process. Our experiences with animals, the elephants for example, and with animal ancestors, let us know that the community is larger than we have ever imagined. Recognizing this, we begin to search out ways to consciously sit in council together, and to form alliances for the sake of the future.)

(I am still speaking here of the motivation for this essay that was a letter and has become a book.)

Finally, I have been enjoined to study the Maya, the great shaman-astronomers of the ancient world whose observations, without telescopes, until recently rivaled our own. I have been taken by contemporary speculations about the end date of the Maya Long Count calendar of December 21, 2012.§ Is this date merely the beginning of another calendar cycle, or does it mark one ending of the world as we know it? Does the end date herald the possibility of a new cycle beginning? For myself, I have taken the date into my heart as a grave reminder that every single activity and gesture needs to be focused toward the task of restoration and how little time we have to change our ways of living.

 C/3

When I started writing this, I did not know to or for whom I was writing, whether it would be to friends or strangers, or whether it was to the spirits themselves. Is it possible that the explicit meanings mask another level of communication in other languages altogether to call forth or encourage the profound and non-literate creatures, the ancestors, even the elementals who have not to this date, despite their undeniable intelligence and spiritual development, been able to prevent human beings from bringing the world to this brink of destruction?

C/3

Alliances of all sorts are on my mind. Spontaneous alliances and matrices, coming into bloom and falling away. This is the way of creation, is it not? These images have gripped me in the last months. They are the inevitable development, over the years, of imagining Councils of Elders and envisioning Darés, healing communities based on indigenous wisdom and contemporary vision. Our lives follow a trajectory; one idea or vision leads to another. We are being called in a time of disaster to imagine viable futures, to live according to radical hope.

C/3

Whatever else it is that I write here, there are two things that I feel must be communicated – the sorrow and the possibility. We are in danger. Grave danger. The earth is suffering. Some say it may be lethal. We are responsible.

Yet there are possibilities. Signs, portents and dreams. Let us meet them together, the real and strange possibilities. Let us pay attention to what is speaking to us, to what is inviting us to be awake.

---

§ *Robert Sitler is creating a website with the collaboration of Maya novelist, Gaspar Pedro Gonzalez on 2012. See:* http://www.stetson.edu/~rsitler/OxlajujB'ak'tun/

೭

When I met with the physicians of the AAEM, I began by telling them my heart is broken. If I forget this for a moment in the attempt to write about it, then I am not speaking what is in my heart.

೭

Nothing about the world I/we inhabit resembles the world I once knew even though I was born in the year of Kristallnacht and the Spanish Civil War – splintered glass and blood. Nothing about the world, its horrors or beauty seems comprehensible any longer – we have passed too far away from what we once called, with much pride, the human. On a daily basis, we are immersed in events that we have called inhuman or unimaginable. Now, the wondrous, kind, compassionate, conscious, ethical activities, formerly innate to the species, are increasingly rare and unusual. We once relied on kindness (and not only that of strangers) and now...? Daré was imagined to correct this – to find a form for people to gather together in consciousness and reflexive kindness. But Daré is only one answer and we have no desire to create a fixed form or ideology. For this reason, we are looking for all the stories, dreams, calls and visions that can lead us back to a world that is safe and generous for all beings.

೭

For the first time, in writing an essay rather than fiction, I do not know where I am going, what I will say, what will be said through me, or where we will be at the conclusion. I only know that certain events and experiences insist that they be written and that great mysteries as well as nightmares are coming to the fore. I have been thinking, wordlessly, about this for months.

If you imagine this essay as a book in miniature, you will be comfortable reading it slowly. There will be time and space to transmit what is coming through and time to take it in and reflect on it.

೭

I begin with this:

There is nothing I know. But there are a few things that lie in a direction that may, perhaps, be useful for us to contemplate. Tentativeness at such times may be a virtue.

This is one of them: Many events and experiences that we would normally regard as discrete, separate, complete unto themselves, request being presented in relationship to each other. One night, listening to jazz, I witnessed two trumpet players call each other forth, raising the ante of each other's skill and genius through a daring display of their individual gifts. It was not competition; it was challenge sliding into invitation. They would not have reached such beautiful extremities without each other.

ఌ

I get the elk skin drum and call to the spirits. When we really need the gods to come, there are no words for it. Then the eagle bone whistle beseeching. Extreme remedies. This admission. Desperate medicine. Prayer.

There were two eagle bone whistles; one is on the altar. The first I sent to Mike Wimberly whose great grandmother had been an Indian princess and his great grandfather had been the son of an African chief. His grandmother was, like her mother and father, enslaved. Imagine it – the ongoing, exhausting, wearying, painful, demeaning extent of slavery day after day from birth to death. The two women, mother and daughter, only spoke to each other in front of white people in bird whistles. I do not think they spoke this way to hide their intentions alone but also to call the bird spirits to them for guidance and protection.

When he received the whistle, after telling the story, something happened – he felt even more deeply connected to the ancestors, as were we. Eagle called him (and us) forth.

On the altar above my desk, a peace eagle carved from turquoise is at the vanguard. Alongside it is the eagle whistle. At the heart's center is the old gray thighbone of an elephant. Behind the eagle is a portion of the brain of an elephant with a spirit figure painted on it by a Masai shaman who knew the songs.§ Whale carved from lapis, buffalo, horse,

---

§ *Just before I returned to Botswana in 2005, a woman contacted me with a request regarding an elephant. Many years ago, at a flea market, she had come upon a hollowed out foot of an elephant made into a household container. She had kept it as a sacred object, but she was moving and downsizing and needed it to have another home. Having read about the Ambassador, she asked me if I would accept it. It arrived within days of my journey and I have made an altar for it. Similarly, I was given a necklace of elephant ivory, not as a piece of jewelry, but to wear as a talisman or sacred ritual object on behalf of the animals.*

frog, wolf, bear, ape, lion, elk, spider, owl, snake. There is a Bushman carving of an elephant, a gift given to me by Vetkat and Belinda Kruiper as a gift in Botswana at the threshold of our pilgrimage to reunite with the Ambassador. The spirit fetishes are aligned, poised, moving without moving, beginning a journey we can only take together. When you pause before these figures, you can see that, despite the horror of this time, anything is possible. Indigenous knowledge and wisdom traditions can arise to sustain us.

ॐ

The Kogi first came to me in a dream when I was in South Africa for the first time. So realistic was the dream that I knew it was a visitation from a people that had, for centuries, traveled across the world in the dreamtime to make spiritual alliances with other shamans and medicine people. But recently, simultaneous with their premonitions about the fate of the earth, they have found fewer people among us, the Younger Brothers, with whom they can commune.[ix]

ॐ

"For four centuries [The Elder Brothers], the last surviving high civilization of pre-conquest America, have watched in silence from their hidden world in the mountains of Columbia. They have kept their world alive and intact, and kept their distance. Now, in what they fear may be the closing days of life on earth, they have summoned us to listen.

"... The Elder Brothers believe that they are the guardians of life on earth. They see the world as a single living being that they have to look after and care for. Their lives are dedicated to nurturing the flora and fauna of the world; they are, in short, an ecological community whose morality is wholly concerned with the health of the planet. Now, the Elder Brothers have seen the changes start which mark the end of life. The world is beginning to die. They know that we are killing it. That is why the Elder Brothers have spoken. They wish to warn us and to teach us."[x]

ॐ

"I [Alan Ereira] can no longer think of the Sierra as a place, distinct form the rest of the world, cut off and separated.

... Just as the world of *aluna* is a spirit-world mirroring every-thing material, so the world of the Sierra mirrors the planet; it is the Heart of the World. If the Sierra is dying, it is because the world is dying."[xi]

ↄ

I didn't stay nine years in dark solitude as the Kogi Mamas do in order to be initiated. And certainly, I didn't spend thirty-six years in the dark being educated only by the spirits, as their Moros do. The latter are the highest developed elders of the Kogi and the ones who, without any contact with us, recognized what we, the ones they call The Younger Brothers, are doing to the earth. I was there in the cave, in silence only for a week but it was enough to be connected to a long line of seers on behalf of the Earth.

As I set out from the hotel after the first night of driving, on the way to the cave, I pulled the Vision Quest card (related to the Hanged Man) from the Vision Quest deck:

"Initiation – meditation – surrender – change of values, beliefs, viewpoint, new outlook. Sincere search for meaning."[xii]

The text spoke of how difficult it is let go of the past, of all the old structures, that is, of our ideas and opinions, because the familiar makes us feel safe. Nevertheless the card was calling the recipient to a Vision Quest and such a journey requires that one offer oneself entirely. Nothing can be withheld when we go to the spirits in this way. The call was to honor the spiritual path before me and to step entirely into the unknown. "...The unknown flings the doors of our perception wide open."

A few hours later near Holbrook, just south of the Navajo reservation, I found myself within an inexplicable story that would be strange enough if it had been a dream. It occurred at the very threshold of the Vision Quest.

Driving in the left lane, I was overtaken, before being able to change lanes, by a white truck without any markings that swung wildly in front of me. Hand scrawled on the back in black felt pen was an arrow ↓ pointing to the name **ODIN**.

Disbelieving, I reached for the tarot deck and pulled a card that I did not look at until I pulled up to a convenience store. Then I went into the store for coffee, a break from the strain of the road and a moment to gather myself after the unfathomable event on the highway.

When I emerged, I saw a man walking from the highway and I knew he was walking to me. I thought, "That is a brother." When we were face to face, he greeted me in Navajo and then asked me if I am a native. "In my heart," I answered. He acknowledged me by saying, "Diné," implying we are from the same tribe. Then he asked me if I could assist him. He wanted a ride to Las Vegas west of us while I was traveling east. I was relieved because I couldn't easily refuse him but I had already entered into silence. Then he asked for some money and I gave him the $9 change I had in my hand.

He thanked me and I drove the car behind the store to look out onto a green field brightened with clusters of brown-eyed susans. Further unnerved, but not knowing entirely why, I took the Haindl deck by Rachel Pollock and asked, "Who is this Navajo man?"

A card leaped out of the deck and fell to the floor. The card was the Father of Cups. In this deck, the Father of Cups is Odin. And in this deck, the Hanged Man of the Grand Arcana is also Odin.

> "…one-eyed Odin hanging on the World Tree for nine days and nights, 'myself sacrificed to myself,' in order to bring up the Runes from the dark well of Mimir."[xiii]

It was then that I looked at the card I had pulled in the car while driving – Ace of Air:

> "Inspiration – divine coincidence – higher insight. By trusting hunches and inner revelations and faithfully acting on them, you are led to your own true self quite easily."[xiv]

My Native American brother, the augury tells me, is Odin. A few weeks later in August, Amanda Foulger,[§] the shaman who first accompanied us when we met the Ambassador, will cast the Runes to help me understand this event.

---

§ *To contact Amanda Foulger, email AFoulger@aol.com. Her current exploration, among others, is the Shaman's Heart.*

I will ask three questions: Why did the Kogi call? Why Odin? What do the spirits want? To the question, why Odin, I will receive what Amanda calls Odin's rune, the gift rune.

She will speak of "a spiritually engineered moment that while brief is irrefutable. An exchange needs to happen and there is a price for what is given and received. Odin," she will say, "is a shaman, poet, singer, bard, the great diviner. He gave his eye and got the Runes, the living symbols of ancient power, the deep language of the universe, the way of divination."

I get on the freeway but I am too agitated to continue. At the first exit, I turn around and return to the place where I met "Odin." I had a $100 bill in my wallet. Yes, there he was waiting for a ride to take him west. I parked the car and walked up to him and said, putting my hand on his heart, "Don't ask me anything. But follow the old ways." I gave him the money. He blessed me in Navajo. We parted.

I understood, however, that I couldn't make this request of him unless I had committed myself as well. In asking him to follow his tradition, I was making a commitment to the Divine to follow the old wisdom ways as well.

On the freeway going east again, a white car swung in front of me in the manner of the white truck. The license plate said VALERIE. I had never seen a license plate like this. It had no other markings. Driving to Arizona some months earlier Valerie Wolf, dear friend, colleague, spirit sister, had come upon an unmarked truck that had scrawled on the dusty exterior: "Deena Follow Me".

Like Amanda Foulger, Valerie Wolf [§] is a remarkable shaman and is also a dreamer. She will be one of those who will be present when the Ambassador will come again in September. She will be able to track what is occurring among all of us by following the connections between her dreams and what occurs with the elephants.

When I telephoned her, she said that Ralph Blum [xv] attributes the blank rune to The Unknowable. The God Odin.

"This sign is entirely about a vision quest and giving oneself entirely to the Divine," she said.

[§] *To contact Valerie Wolf about dreams, dreaming, shamanic practices, bringing back the old ways, shamanic school, email: turtlewolf@charter.net.*

When Valerie's name appeared on the road, I understood then, but not as completely as I do now as I am writing this, that Valerie is the quintessential example in my life of someone who was explicitly called by Spirit and who spent seven years in initiation, learning to follow the old ways and being instructed in the ways of a dream shaman and medicine woman. It seems in these times that Spirit itself organizes what the chiefs and medicine people once organized. Now, so many of us learn what is fundamental to the path without necessarily being called to following the orthodoxy of a particular tradition. I have myself been called in this way and have, as well, been educated and trained as a medicine woman by Spirit through guiding Valerie and others.

Some years ago, Valerie approached me in a formal and traditional manner and asked me to be her teacher. I could not refuse even though I did not know how I would meet what was being asked. Alongside each other, we were both educated by the spirits. In accepting the mandate, I drew on what had transpired in my sixtieth year that I had devoted to becoming an elder to meet the circumstances of these times. I did this though there were then no contemporary models or teachers to assist me. However, like Valerie, I had imagined elders from what I knew about various indigenous cultures and offered myself to the spirits and ancestors for guidance and teachings. When she asked me to be her teacher, I knew I was, yet again, asking to be taken even further into initiation.

Two days later in the cave, I would reread *The Elder Brothers* and remember that the Mamas work entirely through divination.

"Divination is a formalization of the link between the world of *aluna* and the physical world. … It is the reading of signs. To put a question is an act in *aluna*, an act of pure thought, and if it is properly put then its answer is instantaneously present, here in the physical world as well. Divination is the mental process of properly shaping a question, and the highly formal process of reading an answer." [xvi]

For the rest of the drive to Embudo, New Mexico I contemplated what it means to receive a sign. I formulated questions that I would address first to myself and then to others.

If you receive a sign, how then, will you live? What actions will you take, or what path will you enter, that you wouldn't have taken otherwise? To what life and activities is the sign calling you?

In the cave, I wrote in my journal:

Maybe rain will come. The wind is freshening and there are dark patches in the increasingly graying sky. There are the crows by the river that I cannot hear because of the incessant traffic on the highway going to and from Taos. It never stops, not even at night, here at this remote and isolated place of retreat in the hills. Sometimes a car from somewhere unfathomable lights up the mountain road entrance to this little valley of several houses and a cave.

I have reached an impasse or a caesura even as something becomes clear. The Kogi do not ask if they are effective in their work in *aluna* to protect the heart of the world. They have been doing the work for centuries and will continue to do it until they die out. That is, until we kill them and ourselves. They know the consequences of not doing it – the heart of the world will die. They do not speculate on the efficacy of their work and what doing it accomplishes and, at the moment, while the heart of the world is threatened it is still intact. The threat has nothing to do with them but only with us. So they do their work. Once they could make rain fall but they cannot do it for the world because of the extent of the devastation we have inflicted that results in drought in one area and torrential rains in others.

…I am trying to understand the path. Understanding comes from the circumstances that brought me here: Divination is the way of the Kogi. Divination is a conversation that asks for and yields to Divine guidance. This is what we are being called to.

If you receive a sign, how then, will you live? What actions will you take, or what path will you enter, that you wouldn't have taken otherwise? To what life and activities is the sign calling you?

The questions stayed with me in the cave. Six months later, writing this, I think again of the Vision Quest card and the Hanged Man. What indeed happened? Who have I become? Was I initiated? Did I surrender? Have I changed values and beliefs?

When I came home, I read four sentences to Michael from my journal:

> I am leaving the culture. I am stepping out of it. In the choice between serving what humans think serves them and serving the earth, there is no longer a choice. A new meaning of Earth First.

Then I shared the ideas that came to me while I was there:

> To be with Spirit and to pray and act on behalf of the Earth or creation takes precedence over everything else.
>
> My/our task, like the Kogi's sacred task, is to pray for and act on behalf of the earth. It is our task to keep it alive. We are being asked to live our love of the Earth passionately.
>
> The human does not take priority. Neither the human nor the humans we favor. Creation takes precedence.
>
> One does the sacred work without asking if it is effective just as the Kogi Mamas do not ask if their work of keeping the earth alive is effective.
>
> Divination is the process of being in a conversation with Spirit. Prayer is the same.
>
> We may not truly understand what Spirit is asking of us unless we withdraw from the world and its seductions.

❧

Five times in six weeks, the last two in the Cave, I received Hexagram 43: Deciding and Parting[xvii] §

"Deciding and Parting refers to making known an oracular message or pronouncement or notifying the ancestor at the Earth Altar of an important move. ... It includes the idea of parting with the past through the image of rivers separating, and a decisive moment, a critical time for a breakthrough. ...The figure is centered on signals and words, a messenger announcing the results of an oracle. ...It further suggests bringing something dangerous to light, opening and cleansing a wound, a critical announcement in the King's court. This is the arrival of a message from heaven, a fate or mandate. It challenges us to respond fully, quickly and decisively to make the spirit known.

"Deciding/Parting describes your situation in terms of resolutely confronting difficulties. The way to deal with it is to clarify what you must do and act on it, even if you must leave something behind. Move quickly."

All the auguries pointed in the same direction as I had written in my journal:

The directions from the Kogi to the world are clear: Change. They spoke to us and then they locked the gates again.

Though the Kogi have withdrawn, they know that their lives are linked to ours. The Sierra cannot survive if the rest of the natural world continues to be undermined. The Sierra will not be a tiny mountain island of beauty and harmony if the rest of the world goes under. And, if somehow the Sierra remains a fertile area when the surrounding land becomes desert, the younger brother will certainly invade, kill or enslave the Elder Brothers and take the land for themselves – the younger brother has been doing this forever.

§ *All references to the I Ching are from the remarkable translation and interpretation* Total I Ching, Myths for Change, *by Stephen Karcher. One can enter into a profound dialogue with this augury and its foremost interpreter by going to* www.greatvessel.com.

When I came home, I read of the invasion of the Sierra by the military, defoliating the land where they claim coca is being grown for export. The Kogi do use coca, it is essential to their ritual practice, but they do not market it because it is sacred. As a result of the chemical assault, the Kogi children are becoming ill. The crops are failing. The drug lords and the armies fight and the land dies.

I am trying to listen as I am writing, hoping, that as with the Kogi, the spirits will speak to me in this cave or in this silence away from human speech.

There is some way that I have to step away from the culture altogether while living within it. I have to disentangle from its seductions. So, perhaps I, we, are being asked to retreat when we can to protect the heart and body of the world in our own space whatever they may be.

After the threat of rain, the blackened sky is blue again and the half moon white overhead. Whatever story the clouds are telling to those who once could read such sagas is hidden from me except I think the vanguard of storm clouds, those advancing javelins, lances, spikes and spears, are the thunderbeings come to set the world right in their fierce ways. I take a cue from Joanna Macy, "*Dorje.* – Thunderbolt; the ritual implement representing compassion in action," she writes in *Widening Circles.* The sky isn't as pristine, as white, as blue, at home in Topanga. Here the clouds are white and luminescent until the sun goes down and then they are tinted by the entire rainbow of light. I have been trying to read the patterns as the clouds go by. They rarely stay long enough for something to be deciphered. Or they fade. Or they dissolve.

Native peoples have known how to read such signs, and what it means to be in right relationship to the earth. They recognize the sacred and know how to meet it appropriately. I believe we can make alliances with the indigenous people who are left on the planet. I believe some of them are here because they remember. I begin to think that we can communicate with other beings, with non-human beings. The I Ching advises, "Gathering Them." I have been gathering a group of people to meet the Ambassador even though he is an elephant in the wild without email, telephone, or appointment books. *From an unpublished letter to Joanna Macy, March 2005.*

But Spirit has come in these last days again and again speaking in augury, as it does to the Kogi, and speaking in light as it has spoken to me for many years now.

I ask a question and the answer is Hexagram 51 Shake. [xviii] It is an exact instruction and I settle down to meditate upon its direction and implication.

"Shake [xviii] is rain and the spirit that brings the spring rains, violent thunder from beneath that rouses all to new growth after the dead time of winter. Shake/Rousing describes your situation in terms of a disturbing and inspiring shock. The way to deal with it is to rouse things to new activity. Re-imagine what you are confronting. Let the shock shake up your old beliefs and begin something new..."

And then, though there was no sign or indication previously, there was a startling flash of lightning that illuminated the cave through the skylight that is flush with the mountain that contains the cave, followed immediately by a deep, rolling clap of thunder. The fertilizing shock. How can one persist in doubt?

"Four of Stones: The Power of the Earth and Shake/Rousing"

A Prose Poem, March 2005

In a moment of despair, the augury speaks of the power of the earth. On this day, after incessant rains wore away the ground the way misery and fear erode the heart, the sweet waters, grim with debris, muddied, continued their way to the ocean, oily dark, unsafe, no longer the one we were traveling toward, no longer the water we dreamed as sanctuary to everything that lives.

We go where we have to go. Water flows downhill and cannot stop itself even if it can see from its snowy vantage that it will soon be at one with the dolphins beaching themselves and the hapless grebe sticky with tar. Pure, white, icy, it comes from afar, from the snowfields and the translucent glaciers shining with first light, and descending, helpless, bound to us, comrades in a chain gang, hitting the damned hammer of itself into the hapless earth, again and again.

Knowing gloom as the great enemy of possibility, I clutch the tree we still call Hecate, an old one, that could have, like its companion, plummeted, but hasn't plunged into the ravine as great rocks tumble from the escarpment. The tree's gnarled root extends itself into the emptiness, a green figure, surprisingly a girl, a dryad on a tightrope, balancing against all odds.

I grasp the tree and beg for wisdom, imagining across the entire expanse of America, the dispirited dolphins singing a song the winds carry westward while my song too is halting and rough on these lungs filling with salt water. Gaining hope from their own music that somehow we hear and learn and carry, they turn eastward to some new depths, tsunamis open that will refresh them even so. A spirit shakes me, a wave breaking, dashing me to the grassy ocean floor before I can rise in a cetacean spin to the surface and breathe. I do not name what I do not understand.

Then I come home, righting the bluebird house that fell over in the wind, see the wolves gracefully lounging across the threshold, enter, throw the windows open, observe the first fly, spider, moth, lizard, all so young, beginners at this life, carrying, who knows what wisdom age cannot imagine as they scamper delighted and oblivious through this sudden new day.

This is when the augury comes: Four of Stones: The Power of the Earth and also Shake/Rousing. I do not know yet what it says, having paused to write first what it is certain to address, perhaps to ease. Healing it all, now, would be too much to ask.

An ancient tree roots in the underworld and branches in heaven.

Thunder is a great shock coming from beneath,

The rousing sun, green, wood, spring's beginning,

Waking the sleeping insects.

The power of the earth is the voice of God.

Fear is inevitable before the hurricane and the tree of vision.

The omen speaks: Re-imagine and begin again,

The old ones have known this ten thousand years.[xix]

The presence of God will not save us but it will save the world. The mountain rises out of the magma. The melting ice refreshes the sea. We do not know the Earth's future uses of the oils that spew upward through the cracks in the earth. Before the skies darken, a thousand new effulgent greens burnish in the Hiroshima light of the setting sun.

A long sleep is inevitable. A coma of time stretches before us. Then they will come again, the small ones, born of fathers and mothers we will never know. Shapes we do not recognize chattering in unknown languages in our dreams of an incomprehensible future. They are like the lizard, the fly, the moth and the tiniest spider that race in hermetic script across the surface of the mind. Despair disperses in the dust storm and the whirlwind. What more comfort is wanted than that the power of the earth is greater than we?

I fall, one falls down before the earth trembler and the thunder beings, and even in such despair, opens the heart. Then the fog comes in from the sea, a calming poultice for the burning light. The tree holds to its perch like an eagle to its aerie and those trees that fell root deeper into the saturated earth. Languages we have not yet learned come on the wind. Dolphins, far away, leap; we have to know the song is sung to us. Auguries, arrows from another world, strike us awake.

On Friday night, I noticed a menorah in the cave and was called to invite the Sabbath. Lighting the seven candles, I felt great gratitude: "You have always come to me through Light." Suddenly, I had to go outside. The sky was entirely gray before dark. Day was over. Night had fallen. Still, as I was called out, I sat there, meditating, praying. It was then that something happened that was, once again, unexpected and… (I am looking for the right word. Originally, I wrote incomprehensible but it isn't incomprehensible exactly. This essay is being written because we have to recognize that such events are in the realm of the comprehensible and true even if they have been dismissed by the cult of the rational that is also a cult of human domination. It was an event that was unpredictable, outside of human agency. Ah, it was unexpected and awesome. Yes. I have written a chant based on the Hebrew prayer, the *Shechiyanu*: "Awesome Presence, Most Radiant One, thank you for bringing us to this place.")

Presumably it wasn't night yet; presumably it had been so dark only because of the cloud cover. Then the clouds parted and the steep escarpment on the far mountain was illuminated with golden light so exactly that it shone, a golden crown on the sacred land. I asked if I had time to fetch my camera and was, I thought, encouraged and so took the chance. When I returned the crown was still golden and illuminated. Then in an instant the light went out and the night that I thought had already fallen, fell. This occurred on the last night in the cave. The photograph reminds me that the miracle indeed occurred.

There have been signs: What will we do? What actions will we take? What are the signs calling us to?

☙

As I have said, the entire time in and surrounding the cave, I was in the purview of the Hexagram 43: Deciding and Parting.

Sitting with the hexagram and the experiences of that week, I came to understand that Spirit comes to those who listen.

I thought I was being asked to choose between Spirit and the ways of the world, but this is not a choice between Spirit and the world. It is a choice between Spirit and the violent, destructive and cruel ways of the dominant global culture, of the ones the Kogi call the Younger Brothers.

In that cave, I was asked to make an indissoluble alliance with Earth as the place where the spirits congregate. To encourage me or seal a covenant, I was given a sign.

☙

During those weeks I was also preparing to return to Botswana to see the Ambassador. Again and again when I asked, the divination I received from the I Ching regarding the Ambassador was Gathering Them/Great Works, Hexagram 45: [xx]

"Gathering them describes your situation in terms of collecting and gathering. The way to deal with it is to unite people and things through a common feeling or goal. Concentrate the crowd and turn it into an organized whole. This is pleasing to the spirits. This is the time for great projects.

"Common labor coming to expression. Proceed step by step. First things meet in pairs, then they assemble. Gathering Them means assembling and reuniting."

And so we gathered. Michael and I. Cynthia Travis who founded **everyday gandhis** to inspire and document peacebuilding activities in West Africa came with us and brought a team: Bill Saa and Tornorlah Varpilah, peacebuilders from Liberia both, like Cyndie, profoundly concerned with restoring the environment in Liberia that has been entirely devastated by civil war, Andre Lambertson, an African American award winning photographer from New York and Paul Lynch, a videographer who had worked in Gaza, Mozambique and in Sri Lanka after the Tsunami.

Michael Ortiz Hill is the author of several books including *Dreaming the End of the World: Apocalypse as Rite of Passage* and *Gathering in the Names* [with Augustine Mandaza Kandemwa] reissued in 2006 as *Twin from Another Tribe* by Quest Books. Following a dream, Michael went to Zimbabwe where he was initiated as a *nganga* in the water spirit tradition by Shona *nganga* Mandaza Kandemwa. This followed lengthy studies of dreams and, in particular, dreams of apocalypse and dreams of white people about black people and black people's dreams about white people. Because of his first journey to Africa and its aftermath, we were able to introduce the concept of Daré to North America. http://www.gatheringin.com

Cynthia Travis and Bill Saa are partners in **everyday gandhis** (see http://www.everydaygandhis.org). It was through Bill's indigenous understanding of Cynthia's dreams that they re-introduced the traditional Mourning Feast in Liberia as a ritual of reconciliation that allows for the dead to be properly buried so that peace might return to the country. Following the old ways of honoring and burying the dead, "helping the dead cross the river" has become a central ritual, supported by the government, the UN peacekeeping force, several NGO's and the diverse ethnic and religious communities of Liberia. We mention this here as a sign of hope in a desperately wounded land and to emphasize the real assistance and insight that dreams can provide.

William Saa, peacebuilder-in-residence at **everyday gandhis** explains the importance of the mourning feasts and their role in ending violence:

"What is a traditional mourning feast?

"At the core of the traditional mourning ceremony of crossing the river, the family and community gather to honor the dead with a feast. At the center of the feast is the common bowl from which we eat. The common bowl reminds us each day, as well as on the day of mourning, that we are nourished by our common life. On the feasting day of mourning, everyone also comes before the common bowl. Before we take our food, we know we must be pure of heart and ready to eat with everyone who is there. We recognize each other's pain and loss. This recognition is the first act that leads to forgiveness. Thus, we have a long and honorable tradition that in its simple and beautiful way supports the family and the community and heals what has been injured. Our feasting tradition of mourning is also a way of peacemaking as we settle our disputes and resolve our conflicts. Why is it important?

"As a result of civil war, over 350,000 Liberians died either by a direct bullet, silent weapon, disease, or starvation. Some died in the bushes and some died underwater. Some have no graves. Some were dumped in mass graves. We have had no proper funeral ceremonies for most of our loved ones who died during this terrible war period.

"Due to the long war, we have not been able to engage in the mourning process or ceremonies that have always been used by our different tribal groups.

"For the sixteen tribes of Liberia, who believe that there is a life after death, the exact rituals of mourning are very important. After a person dies, it is essential for the living to assist that person in "crossing the river." Crossing the river helps the dead reach their ancestors who have passed away before them. The dead cannot reach the ancestors without our ritual help. In the traditional way of feasting and prayer, the living and the dead are unified and in harmony with each other." (See http://www.everydaygandhis.org/feasting-doc.html)

Tornorlah Varpilah was just appointed Deputy Minister for Planning, Research and Human Resource Development in the Ministry of Health and Social Welfare in the new government of Liberia. In Botswana and later in Liberia, he was concerned with helping to establish early warning systems regarding danger and violence based on insights, dreams and observations from *zoes* [shamans, healers, medicine people] and other members of the community. Recognizing that many women of Liberia had dreamed the war before it happened, and many people, including Tornorlah himself, were "protected" by information derived from dreams and intuitions, the hope is that revaluing the old forms will recreate the old alliances with Spirit to protect the country from another such bloody war. One of the concerns of Tornorlah and **everyday gandhis** is that the *zoes* and medicine people rely on signs from the animals, as all indigenous people do, to inform them of the condition of the world. Liberia, like all the countries that have experienced modern warfare, has a devastated environment and the animals are being hunted for food as well as having their habitat encroached upon. **everyday gandhis** is committed to illuminating the relationship between peacebuilding and the environment and supports indigenous efforts to assist restoration.

For information on Andre Lambertson see http://www.digitaljournalist.org/issue0004/andreintro.htm.

Paul Lynch interviewed the American woman peace protester, Rachel Corey, who was killed by an IDF bulldozer, which ran her over during the demolition of a Palestinian house at the Rafah refugee camp in the southern Gaza Strip. He was the one who was called to identify her body.

Also with us was Valerie Wolf, Charlene Hollis from South Africa, and two Bushmen writer-artist activists from the Kalahari who are trying to sustain and encourage the children and adults of a decimated people. *(See* http://www.vetkat.co.za/*)*

This excerpt is from an email that arrived today Wednesday, February 11, 2006 from Charlene as I was working on this paragraph in order to introduce everyone: "My daughter, Maya and I have moved our life to Cape St. Francis on the East coast of Southern Africa.... Much awaited us here! Yesterday Maya was on the beach ... a baby dolphin was struggling in the waves. She picked it up to put it deeper into the ocean, unsuccessfully.... We went to help... five local people...eventually, after a few hours, she gave up and landed on the beach, we covered her with a wet t-shirt and I gave Reiki while the National Sea Rescue Boat waited behind the waves. A neighbor ran for his paddle ski. Lifting her gently onto the ski, she was paddled intrepidly beyond the surf to the rescue boat then they zoomed off to follow a pod of dolphins at the Seal Point. She was accepted by them and off she went! ... Juliette and I have invited Belinda and Vetkat to be here with us.... And we are aiming to hold an exhibition for Vetkat. Lots of dreams going back and forth between the Kalahari and Cape St Francis!! Fire and Water!! Kalahari having strange weather. Extremely hot then big rains?!?"

In the way that everything is connecting to everything else, at this last moment of copyediting what I hope is the final manuscript, I was forwarded an email from a woman named Linda Seagraves whom I had had the occasion to introduce to Charlene, Belinda and Vetkat. What follows are some excerpts from Linda Seagraves' temporary website set up to chronicle her journey to South Africa for Stephen Karcher's College of Diviners:

"When South Africans speak of the nine recognized, indigenous tribes living in the country today, the Bushmen are conspicuously absent from the roster of Zulu, Xhosa, Sotho, Ndebele, Swazi, Venda, Pedi, Tswana and Shangana. In the eyes of many, they are extinct... a people who simply do not exist. Of those South Africans who do recognize their existence, the Bushmen are not afforded the exalted, romanticized, status bestowed upon them by western spiritual groups. Rather, they are the reviled, the exiled, ... human refuse confined to reservations and plagued by poverty, illiteracy and alcoholism.

"In the words of a new friend that I would meet on the journey:

'The Bushmen ... were once very numerous, and roamed the whole of South Africa... the evidence remains in the numerous rock paintings that they left behind them. By right of occupation, the land was theirs. But because they put up no visible signs of settlement, their right was not recognised. As their land was invaded by Black herdsman and White settler, they retreated further and further south and east, into the desert and mountain regions. They were a peace-loving people who would rather flee from confrontation than resort to violence... There were terrible massacres, atrocities on both sides. The Bushmen were regarded as vermin, beasts to be destroyed without mercy. Even babies were murdered with the rest. Those Bushmen who survived the carnage became a displaced people... With all their land taken, they existed as squatters on the land of others, finding survival as best they could. They intermarried with the local Blacks and Coloureds, hid their origins, forgot their language. The songs died and the stories vanished. To be a Bushman was such a stigma that it was better to hide it.

'... All the Bushmen ever wanted was to be left alone to live the life that suited them — walking the dunes, hunting and gathering, singing, dancing, painting and telling stories. Ownership was a foreign concept to them. Belonging made the world theirs. They didn't need to possess anything, because they were connected in spirit to everything around them... The world has never been able to understand a people who strive for nothing, who don't need to own or possess anything, who live by different values...'

"As I made my way across South Africa, I would be strangely plagued and haunted by the story of the Bushmen whose 'stone age ancestors were the first human beings to walk the earth.' Their story and that of another displaced people, the Maasai of East Africa, would resonate in my heart and mind, conscious and otherwise with every step that I took across the continent.

"On my third day in Cape Town, Charlene called to ask if I might want to see a film on Kenya's Maasai warriors at the World Cinema Festival being held in Cape Town that same week. She was particularly excited because her friend Miyere Ole Miyandazi Selenguironeirei, a Maasai warrior would be joining us at the theatre. Miyere had become a local legend... He had walked 2,551 miles from Kenya to South Africa, across Tanzania, Zambia and Botswana to draw attention to the plight of the Masaai, an indigenous tribe engaged in a bitter land dispute with the Kenyan government over what many believe is the theft of their ancestral land.

"In Miyere's words as expressed in the South African press:

'I left Kenya in August, traveling through several African countries without a passport, to bring to the attention of the world the abuse of the word democracy in Kenya, and that the ancient Maasai people don't have a voice. We have been ruthlessly exploited by tourists and corrupt government officials who view the Maasai as a backward, exotic group. As Maasai we lacked nothing in the bush, our cattle mean everything. They [colonialists] take away the land, then buy our cattle at cheap prices. We are nomads, but have a huge land problem. Without land, you can't have cattle. Without cattle, we cannot survive. I have come specifically to Cape Town, which is recognised throughout the continent as an international meeting place, to make it known that the Maasai are demanding that our culture be respected...'

"The historical record shows that in 1904, the British entered into a contract with the Maasai to lease 2,000,000 hectares, (approx. 7,772 sq. miles), of their ancestral land on the Laikipia Plateau for 100 years. With the backdrop of snow capped Mount Kenya, the Laikipia Plateau in central Kenya is the last stronghold of romantic

East Africa where vast open ranches have been transformed into game reserves and now contain some of the most exclusive tourist lodges in the remotest parts of Kenya. The lease expired in 2004, but the Kenyan government, which took over the contract from the British after independence, now claim that the lease was for 999 years. With a tourist industry heavily reliant on the world famous Maasai Mara and Serengeti game reserves, (formerly Maasai grazing land where 75% of Kenya's wildlife can be found), it is small wonder that the Kenyan government covets the Masaai ancestral lands.

"The Maasai have been arrested, shot at and persecuted for allowing their cattle to graze on the disputed land. The Maasai respond, '...The lease has expired. We want our land back.' On his 6 month journey of protest, Miyere survived by eating roots and plants, and suffered a series of natural and human catastrophes, including narrowly escaping being trampled by a herd of elephants when he swam across a river between Zambia and Botswana. Interestingly, Miyere never carried a passport. Upon reaching border crossings, he simply said: 'I am a Maasai. We are nomads. How can we have passports?'

"Several days following the Maasai film and meeting Miyere, Belinda Kruiper arrived in Cape Town from her home in the Kalahari Desert. She had made a special effort to arrive before my departure the next afternoon. At first glance, Belinda appears delicate and fragile; thin to the point of emaciation. You understand immediately, that hers has been a life of physical deprivation, sacrifice and at times, literal starvation. Despite her physical stature, this woman is tough and a fierce protector of the Bushmen and their legacy.

"There was a collective sigh of relief that the meeting proposed by Deena Metzger would finally take place. Charlene, Belinda and I sat together at an outdoor cafe in Cape Town. An hour into the conversation, we were joined by none other than Miyere, the majestic Maasai. Belinda, an author and poet in her own right, brought with her a portfolio of reproductions of her husband Vetkat's art, called the Sacred Collection, a series of 23 pieces which tell the story of the struggles of the last decade. The original art of this collection considered by Vetkat to be sacred is under the custodianship of the ARA Foundation, organized around the South African concept of Ubuntu, which says that by belonging to a community, the individual becomes strengthened. Vetkat's Sacred Collection is not for sale but, held in trust for the people of the Kalahari.

"In the 1970s, the white South African government forced the Bushmen to leave their ancestral grounds, and for years the Bushmen way of life was thought lost. But a decade ago, the Bushmen reemerged, and Vetkat's community, the Khomani Bushmen began a tough and bitter battle with the South African government. They won their case and the right to return to their land. But political struggle and poverty continued to ravage the community.

"The true victory would come not only in reclaiming the land, but in reclaiming the Bushmen culture and preserving their way of life."

Among other reasons, we had invited the Kruipers because they are of the hunter-gatherer people, the First People who have had the longest and most articulate relationship with the animal world.

Even as we wondered why we were being called to the Elephants and marveled about its possibilities, we realized that each of us had had deep contact with violence and war and so entered into the stories, the truthful and self-scrutinizing conversations between friends that peace-making requires. We told dreams and visions, we spoke of the difficulties, frustrations and contradictions, the failures within ourselves, and the struggles to meet these as the work of making peace.

Vetkat and Belinda Kruiper
Photo © 2006 Andre Lambertson

໑

The Ambassador had come twice, once in 2000 and once in 2001.[xxi] If he were to come again, I wanted it to be witnessed by others who would recognize the implications of such an event for the future of the earth. I also wanted to learn, in community, how we might make real and active alliances with the animals on behalf of the planet. Over the years, the spirits training me to think or see in the old ways required of me the constant undoing of self, of western mind, science, scripture and of will in order to yield to other ways of knowing and to recognize other intelligences than the human in the world.

It seems I am being given a sacred alphabet. I only know some of the words for the letter A: Alliance. Alignment. Affiliation. Attunement.

Attunement. There are those who insist on changing reality and those who attune themselves to it as it is, who align themselves with the nature of reality. And who make alliances for this purpose. They go around with their antenna out looking, seeking, feeling.

Antenna. At Fossil Rim, a preserve for African animals, for research and preservation, Krystyna Jurzykowski, its founder and former director is driving. http://www.fossilrim.com/

We stop. "Look," she says, "the tips of the branches of the trees and the antlers of the antelope ... they extend into the world. That is how they know the world. These are their antennae."

In Joshua Tree, the ocotillo are in bloom. Their red flowers are like the antenna on the antlers of deer and antelope. I am aware of Krystyna's wisdom and presence.

Alliance. I say it again and again. I think of matrices, of the nexus, of the net of Indra, of gatherings, of associations, coalitions, villages, tribes, kinship nets, cooperatives, comings together, common purposes, councils: save creation.

From an unpublished letter to Joanna Macy, March 2005

When he was sixteen, my son, Greg, led me into an alliance with wolf through his familiars Loba and Timber Wolf. Perhaps it was my ongoing relationship with Timber Wolf that brought me to understand that animals are profoundly sensitive and intelligent and can be agents of healing. In the last years, much of the testimony to animal intelligence in the wild has referred to that of dolphins, who, so afflicted by human activity, beach themselves and die in huge numbers and yet regularly assist people in the ocean who would otherwise drown or be injured by sharks.

๛

While indigenous people have recognized the intelligence and spiritual development of animals this has not been obvious to western mind. That animals are involved with creation is an old story that we can read as a myth, as fantasy, or we can understand that myths, like dreams, describe the world as it really is.

From Robert Sitler's unpublished manuscript *The Mayan Road:*

Like most Maya, the Hero Twins grew corn. Being virtually omnipotent, they decided to create two supernatural tools for their agricultural work. One divine twin wielded an axe that could cut a tree with the mere touch of its blade. His brother created a large hoe that automatically removed weeds and prepared the soil. The magical axe and mattock did their work and the twins avoided the physically enduring rigors of mountain corn farming. Hunahpu and Xbalanke enjoyed the day relaxing as the magical implements readied the field for planting. The two feigned hard work in the field to their wise elder grandmother and midwife Xmucane, going so far as to rub dirt on their hands and throw sawdust on their heads as evidence of their labor. The following dawn, when they returned to their corn garden, they found that the forest has somehow completely regenerated and that there was no trace of their cleared field. After complaining to their patiently silent grandmother about what had happened, the Twins sent out their magic farm tools once again, clearing the patch a second time for planting. This time, however, they hid in the brush to see what would happen. *In surprise, they watched as a congregation of every wild animal known to the Maya gathered from the woods and magically recreated the original ecosystem by simultaneously intoning a sacred incantation. The Popol Vuh says "They are the ones who are doing it, all the animals, small and great: puma, jaguar, deer, rabbit, fox, coyote, peccary, coati, small birds, great birds.* xxii [Italics mine] At this point, the Hero Twins vainly tried to capture the animals but every single animal ultimately escaped their grasp, although some, like the rabbit, were permanently deprived of their once-longer tails, snatched off by the Maya heroes. The twins eventually accept defeat, the only time in Mayan mythology that they succumb to a higher power.

In surprise, they watched as a congregation of every wild animal known to the Maya gathered from the woods and magically recreated the original ecosystem by simultaneously intoning a sacred incantation.

ℰↃ

Music, song and incantation are means of restoration and healing. Dreams of singing ourselves and the world back to health abound in Daré as we explore the use of sound to bring healing to each other. For a few years, I have been imagining a Concert of Lost Notes. Recent research reveals that each eco-niche is a universe of sound. When a bird or animal disappears, the environment is unbalanced, as an orchestral piece would be without a certain instrument or theme, and so the creatures who live there lose their way. To serve the earth, I have been asking musicians to carry the song of a creature that has gone extinct, is greatly diminished in its numbers and absent from or in exile from its habitats, and sing it into that void. How do we know but that the animals will resurrect at the sound of their intrinsic beauty as sung back to them?

ℰↃ

The relationship that I had with dogs and wolves was natural to me and I sought it out the way one seeks out friendship. But the elephants came on their own. I have spoken about it this way: The elephants put out a desperate call. Probably many received the call like I did. I didn't know then what was implied, but I answered nevertheless. This was just one event of learning over the years about the reality of the spirit world and the ways that spirit, if invited, may reveal a personal path of benefit for the earth and all its creatures. Indigenous people lived this way for millennia. Sometimes they made mistakes or disregarded the wisdom that was being offered to them. Disaster often followed – as in the end of the classical Maya civilization or the disappearance of the Anasazi. As is happening to us today. Only this time, the entire world is at stake and those few who remain who know the old ways that might save us are as vulnerable to extinction as the elephants and the polar bears.

ℰↃ

The animals gathering at the dry water hole in Hwange, Zimbabwe, occupied first by the great herds of fierce water buffalo, have begun to fight against each other for whatever moisture might be left for them; this behavior is against their nature. We are teaching them violence. Or this is a consequence of how we have destroyed their habitat, their homes, their family and tribal gatherings, their courtship rituals, their little ones, their sacred songs and dances, their constant and unceasing rituals of beauty, their minds and their great spirits. They become breeds they have never imagined or known and do not recognize.

South African Panel Targets "Despicable" Hunting of Animals with No Hope of Escape, by Clare Nullis, Associated Press

CAPE TOWN, South Africa (AP) 10.25.05, 10:00a — Lions bred in captivity to be shot and killed by a pleasure-seeking tourist. Rhinos felled by bow and arrow for fun. Zebras bred with donkeys to slow their escape from hunters.

A panel of experts highlighted the darker side of South Africa's booming wildlife industry Tuesday and recommended a total ban on "canned hunting" — the release of captive-bred animals to be killed for sport with no chance of escaping their human predators.

Environment Minister Marthinus van Schalkwyk said the government would introduce legislation next year to salvage South Africa's reputation as an international haven for wildlife.

"We want to stop the approach of 'anything goes' in terms of hunting and crossbreeding,'' said van Schalkwyk, himself an avid hunter. "Some practices which have been developed over years and decades are distasteful and despicable."

South Africa is famed for its teeming animals and brilliant birds. The jewel in the conservation crown, Kruger National Park, draws millions of camera-toting visitors each year.

But in the shadow of Kruger — where all hunting is outlawed — smaller parks have sprung up, aimed at visitors who carry rifles. Last year, an estimated 6,700 tourists killed nearly 54,000 animals.

Faced with mounting public concern, van Schalkwyk convened a panel of environmental conservation and management experts in April to look into the industry and suggest ways of regulating it.

Documents provided to the panel by the TRAFFIC wildlife trade monitoring network provided details on the extent of the "trophy" hunting business.

It said 190 lions were hunted last year by foreign tourists, worth an estimated $3.3 million — or $17,500 each. Nearly 5,500 kudus — valued at $5.3 million in all — also were killed, along with 45 leopards worth an estimated $250,000.

The list of slain animals included baboons, giraffes, elephants, hippopotamuses, mongooses, porcupines, warthogs and zebras. Prices paid ranged from $25 for the humble pigeon or quail to $25,000 for the mighty white rhinoceros. Some hunters were offered the chance to shoot large mammals, including rhinoceroses, with bows and arrows, condemning them to a long and painful death, the panel found.

"This is something that no civilized country can continue to tolerate," van Schalkwyk said.

To satisfy the insatiable demand of foreign hunters, game parks resorted to importing boars from Russia and tahrs from the Himalayas, the panel said.

Breeders also used crossbreeding and genetic manipulation to make the potential prey more appealing — for instance, by introducing more albino strains in lions. This could have devastating implications for long-term biodiversity in South Africa, the panel said.

One of the most extreme examples quoted was that of the "zonkey," a crossbreed between the fleet-footed zebra and the slower-moving donkey.

The panel concluded that hunting is — and should remain — an integral part of South African life because of its importance to the economy and employment. Hunting kudu and other game to make "biltong" — a popular local dried meat — is one of a number of entrenched traditions, it said.

But the panel said there must be more controls, greater self-regulation and a concerted attempt to transform the white-dominated hunting industry into a multiracial business that benefits more sectors of society.

Crispian Olver, chairman of the expert panel, said implementation of its recommendations would help repair South Africa's tarnished image among environmentalists and animal rights groups.

"We would be able to stand proud among the nations of the world and no longer be ashamed of our hunting," he said.

Get Out Of The Way... He Hasn't Forgotten

By Roger Highfield, Science Editor, Telegraph, UK

http://news.telegraph.co.uk/news/main.jhtml?xml=/news/2006/02/16/weleph16.xml

(Filed: 16/02/2006)

The reputation that elephants have for never forgetting has been given a chilling new twist by experts who believe that a generation of pachyderms may taking revenge on humans for the breakdown of elephant society.

The New Scientist reports today that elephants appear to be attacking human settlements as vengeance for years of abuse by people.

In Uganda, for example, elephant numbers have never been lower or food more plentiful, yet there are reports of the creatures blocking roads and trampling through villages, apparently without cause or motivation.

Scientists suspect that poaching during the 1970s and 1980s marked many of the animals with the effects of stress, perhaps caused by being orphaned or witnessing the death of family members — and producing the equivalent of post-traumatic stress disorder.

Many herds lost their matriarch and had to make do with inexperienced "teenage mothers." Combined with a lack of older bulls, this appears to have created a generation of "teenage delinquent" elephants.

Joyce Poole, the research director at the Amboseli Elephant Research Project in Kenya, who has co-authored a paper on elephant behaviour, said: "They are certainly intelligent enough and have good enough memories to take revenge.

"Wildlife managers may feel that it is easier to just shoot so-called 'problem' elephants than face people's wrath.

"So an elephant is shot without [people] realising the possible consequences on the remaining family members and the very real possibility of stimulating a cycle of violence."

Her study showed that a lack of older bulls to lead by example had created gangs of hyper-aggressive young males with a penchant for violence towards each other and other species. For instance, in Pilanesburg National Park in South Africa, young bulls have been attacking rhinos since 1992.

And in Addo Elephant National Park, also in South Africa, 90 per cent of male elephants are killed by another male — which is 15 times the "normal" figure.

Richard Lair, a researcher specialising in Asian elephants at the National Elephant Institute based in Thailand, said there were similar problems in India, where villagers lived in fear of male elephants, which the villagers claim attack the village for only one reason — to kill humans.

"In wilderness areas where wild elephants have no contact with human beings they are, by and large, fairly tolerant," he said.

"The more human beings they see, the less tolerant they become."

The rains have not come and Robert Mugabe, the President of Zimbabwe, has invited the people to hunt and eat the wildlife that was, until now, somewhat protected if not entirely from poachers hunting ivory, rhinoceros horn or arranging kills of the "big five" for wealthy hunters. The animals attack each other because they fail to recognize themselves or each other. We have done this. We have made war against the natural world and the elements, and as is the way of war, the victims have turned vicious.

Sometimes even scripture reveals the nature of the world and the animals:

From the story of Balaam and the ass.

On the way, the ass manifested every sign of alarm; it swerved suddenly from the path, crushed Balaam's leg against a wall and finally sank to the ground under him, so that Balaam cruelly beat it and even threatened it with death. Then the ass was endowed by God with the power of speech, and upbraided Balaam with his cruelty towards it. At the same time Balaam's eyes were opened and he saw the cause of the ass's strange conduct, *viz.* an angel of the Lord standing in the way with drawn sword to bar his passage. The angel upbraided Balaam with his cruel conduct towards the ass and told him that the action of the ass had saved his life. The angel of the Lord allows him to go on his way with the warning that he not speak anything but what the Lord asks him to speak.

This is the way it is. The animals are alarmed. They may even stampede us in order to stop us. Finally, they collapse with the weight of carrying us where we must not go. They speak up in ways we cannot deny and berate us with our cruelty toward them. And finally we recognize it is God that is standing before us making known our grave cruelties and failures.

❧

Some of us who were born into western mind are wondering if we can claw our way back to the understanding, rituals, visions, life styles that accord with the ways of the spirits who love creation. We cannot do this if we cling to obdurate skepticism and disbelief. Rather, we are being called to cultivate the mind and heart that can discern the presence of divine potential and distinguish between our own thoughts and desires and the call and direction of the spirits. This is most difficult. Ultimately, we are being asked to discern the presence of the divine and acknowledge that the spirits are real.

Chief Phil Crazy Bull came to Michael Ortiz Hill in a dream or visitation on Saturday, March 11, 2006 to speak heartbrokenly about the devastation of the land. He asserted that the thesis of Michael's book *Dreaming the End of the World: Apocalypse as a Rite of Passage* that all would be well if we loved ourselves was not sufficient. Michael responded that this was far from the thesis of the book. Michael said that this book was about facing what European and American culture has done in destroying the world. Chief Crazy Bull then said, "My people have been on this land for a long time. This is where we are from."

In the year 2000, Chief Leonard Crow Dog named Phil Crazy Bull a Chief at Crow Dog's Paradise Sundance in Rosebud, South Dakota. Chief Phil, a Sundancer and Yuwipi Man, was a Lakota medicine man and member of the Thunder Dreamer Society.

Chief Phil's visitation brings up the memory of another dispute around the tree of life which is a theme of this essay and how the interference of the U.S. government foments anger and dispute between indigenous peoples themselves. Once again, we see the theme of the cutting down of the trees emblematic of what is happening to the earth and the people and beings who live here.

Tuesday, September 04, 2001, BIG MOUNTAIN, Ariz.

The Tree of Life at the Navajo Sundance grounds here stood tall, its trunk and branches festooned with colorful prayer bundles filled with tobacco and bits of flesh cut from the dancers' bodies.

That was before Hopi tribal authorities came in two weeks ago with bulldozers and chainsaws, smashing through the cedar arbor that surrounded the dance circle, cutting down the tree, and running it — and its offerings — through a woodchipper. The Sundance ground is on Hopi land.

It was as though, said Navajo Sundancer Vernon Manuelito,

someone went into a Catholic church, took down the crucifix and smashed it. Manuelito was among a handful of people who traveled here Sunday for a ceremony to try to reduce the effects of the tree-cutting.

Twenty years of prayers were burned and sacrificed at that tree, said Chief Phil Crazy Bull, a Rosebud Lakota medicine man who led the ceremony. "All of those were desecrated." ...

Big Mountain is on territory once jointly held by both tribes but split between them by Congress in 1974. Some 12,000 Navajo and 300 Hopi families were resettled as part of that order.

Today, 10 Navajo families remain in what is now Hopi territory, living without electricity or running water on the high-desert hill (Big Mountain is a misnomer) many miles from the nearest paved road. "I was born and raised there. My umbilical cord is buried there. My ancestors survived the Spanish invasion, and the Kit Carson invasion and now their resistance is still going on," said Robert Bennally, whose mother, Louise, still lives on Big Mountain.

"What's peace for the Hopi," he added, "is war for us."

But the Hopi counter ... is that the Navajo's vast reservation was repeatedly enlarged in the late 1800s until it completely surrounded Hopi land.

The tree was cut after repeated warnings by the Hopi to vacate the grounds because it's their land.

A 1996 agreement that was supposed to settle the Big Mountain dispute has not been enforced against the 10 families. "People forget our history," said Wayne Taylor, former Hopi tribal chairman.

...About 20 years ago, some Navajo adopted the Plains tribes' annual four-day ceremony involving sweats, fasting, hours of dancing, and ritual cutting of small bits of flesh. Now there are four Sundance grounds on the Navajo reservation: Little Big Medicine, Survival, Pinon and — until two weeks ago — the Anna Mae camp at Big Mountain, named for Anna Mae Aquash, a Micmac woman and American Indian Movement activist who was found shot to death on the Pine Ridge Reservation in 1976. ... Navajo who have adopted the Sundance have heartfelt beliefs about it. "I carried the canupa (the pipe) into the first Sundance here," said a weeping Donna Johnson, now 31, at Sunday's ceremony on Big Mountain. She stared at the hole where the Tree of Life had stood. "I never expected anything like this. This traumatizes everything — your soul, your spirit."

As Johnson spoke, the scent of burning sweetgrass and fresh-cut sagebrush perfumed the air. Eagle and crane feathers were placed atop rocks at each of the four directions around the tree site. Later, said Crazy Bull, they would be taken to the three other Sundance grounds, with one rock and the white crane feathers returning to South Dakota with him.

∽

In his dissertation, "Through Ladino Eyes: Images of the Maya in the Spanish American Novel" (1994) – that I was led to, also, by mysterious means – Robert Sitler writes:

"...even modern Maya maintain a world view that is quite distinct from that of contemporary Ladinos... [A new point of view] among Western academics ...implies an acceptance of what the Maya call the Otherworld; the invisible realm of non-physical, some would say "magical," experience that is an essential component of the Maya belief system. ...In a recent book that characterizes this new perspective among Mayanists, the anthropologist David Freidel has openly asked us to accept that the Otherworld, the place that "the ancient Maya called *Xibalba*, the 'place of awe,' is real and palpable." He goes on to assert that, "The Maya world . . . is a place of living magic." [xxiii]

I was connected to this dissertation[xxiv] and Robert Sitler through what I must recognize as miraculous means. It opened a door to the Maya for me that wouldn't have been opened otherwise. But, equally mysterious, it provided a means to fathom a dream that came to a member of the Daré community, Maria Pollia who teaches theology and is the campus minister at a Catholic high school in Los Angeles.

"*Huipil* Dream, October 19, 2005

I am standing in front of a modest house covered with vines and foliage. Deena Metzger comes out of the house, and she is wearing a beautiful Guatemalan huipil. I note how beautiful and unusual it is. It has a light blue background and is skillfully woven with very regular geometric shapes in a variety of bright colors. It is different because these garments, which are worn by the indigenous people of Central America, are usually no longer than mid-thigh length. This one is voluminous and reaches to the ground.

Deena points to her left to a round chrome and glass clothing rack, the type that one sees in department stores. It has a single garment hanging on it. It is a shirt that is similar to an American sailor's shirt with the bib in the back, only instead of being navy blue and white, is red with white piping. There is a white star on the left side of the shirt, which would be over the heart. Deena says, "Put it on." I answer, "But Deena, it's too big." "Put it on." Again, I protest that it is too big. She asks me to put it on again, and this time I do. I look down to see that the sleeves are at least 10 inches longer than my arms. I look up at Deena to say, "You see? It's too big."

I look down again, to find to my amazement that the garment has changed completely. It has become a huipil very similar to the one that Deena is wearing, very generously cut, reaching to the ground. Only instead of the geometric design that Deena's has, it is the garden, the jungle, and the rainforest. It is stunningly and so skillfully woven with flowers, vines, butterflies, birds, monkeys and other animals and so on, all the gorgeous variety of creation. I am awestruck and honored to be wearing such a garment.

Then I decide to see what is on the back of it. I look over my right shoulder, and instead of the glorious colors that grace the front the back is a selection of sickly grays, foul browns, dead blacks. I go from looking over my shoulder to seeing the images in front of my eyes. They have the look of an impressionistic oil paint-ing, but they are constantly moving. To my horror, I see bones and skulls emerging out of poisoned soil; there is a putrid black river moving sluggishly through the center of the composition with bod-ies floating in it face down. Inset into this painting of death are three photographs in a terrible sepia tone. One is of overturned cars, the second, a burning city, and the third, a factory with huge smokestacks belching out black, noxious smoke. I am horrified and sickened by these scenes.

I look up at Deena for a moment terrified, and then look over my left shoulder to see what is pictured there. Again, the images are now in front of my eyes. It is still a 'painting' only more distinct, of a more realistic style. It is of a campesino. He is being crucified upside down. His mouth is moving as if he is trying to say some-thing to me, but he gags and cannot speak. He is in shock, terrified and distressed. His eyes, rolling back and forth in his head, plead for me to help him, but I cannot. The pitiful sight of his suffering and my helplessness sicken me.

I look up again at Deena and she says one word to me: 'Chamama'. An indigenous man who is crouching on the ground a few feet away from me on my right stands slowly and with his hand covering his mouth says slowly with great reverence and awe in his voice, "Oh! She has never spoken The Name (and I do not hear but understand telepathically—'of the Witch') before!" (The term 'the Witch' is not pejorative.) There is a sense that the situation has now become so dire that the time has come for this holy name to be invoked.

The dream ends here."

The word in the dream was for us untranslatable for a long time and Maria Pollia concluded that it was the Quechua word *(pa)chamama* — the name of the rift valley in Peru and the Earth Goddess.

However, Robert Sitler wrote: "I can't help but wonder about a Mayan dream using a Kechwa term...*(pa)chamama* ... maybe ... but I can't help but want to go Maya with a Mayan *huipil* dream. For the Mam people (Mam itself is a reference to the ancient ones), *chman* is a reference to the shamans (which some would call "*brujos*", the dream (witches) and to both grandparents and grandchildren."

It astonished, us, of course, that Maria Pollia had dreamed the exact translation into Mayan of the words spoken in her dream.

Later speaking of the dream, Maria Pollia added: "During the consideration of this dream, members of my dream circle commented that the red shirt is similar to the new garment that was put on as the catechumen stepped newly born out of the waters of Baptism. I am reminded by this insight that in the early Church, the rite of Baptism was not merely the public acceptance of a set of beliefs, but was in fact a dangerous act. Christians at that time refused because of the teachings of Jesus, to serve in the Roman legion; this was the actual reason that Christianity was considered a dangerous cult and outlawed. When one was baptized, one was in effect saying, 'I will not serve the Empire!' It was a declaration that meant your life."

Because of our Daré practice of interpreting dreams as sent by the ancestors to the community for the sake of wisdom and guidance, our community has been "carrying" the dream for several months. Because the dream was about a *huipil*, we have called the process of awareness and consciousness, "wearing" the dream. Essentially, in "wearing" the dream we are asking the ancestors or spirits what they want us to know by sending this dream to us through Maria Pollia.

In his dissertation, Sitler is concerned with the patronizing Ladino attitudes toward Mayan culture and spiritual practices as depicted in the novel, among others, *Oficio de Tinieblas* by the Mexican novelist Rosario Costellanos. Aside from appreciating Sitler's alliance with indigenous wisdom, I was astonished to find that the *huipil*, the crucifixion and the living images in Maria Pollia's dream were the focus of derision in that novel, published by Penguin Books in 1998.

പ

Latin America. Africa. How much suffering indigenous cultures and peoples have endured as a consequence of colonization or what we call civilization. The drought in southern Africa and Kenya that leaves animals and people starving to death is mirrored in Liberia by torrential rains. The roads dissolve into deep rivers of impassable mud. The cars pile up on all sides until the UN patrols are themselves mired and call for the one rig, belonging to the UN, to pull them out or until there are enough men to lift the cars out of the mire. Within 25 kilometers of Voinjama on our way to Monrovia we were mired in the mud and walked a mile or two to the village where we spent the night in an entirely bare infirmary. You would not have known from the sweetness that greeted us that the country was a few days from a possibly dangerously contentious election that could reignite the most brutal and violent civil war in the ravaged country mostly without food, electricity, sanitation, social services, health care, hospitals, education that had once prided itself on its development and democratic processes. A country that had said, as we do in the U.S. despite the current vicious assault on democratic processes, "this can't happen here." A country that despite its origins by freed slaves from the United States knows deeply as do the other countries of West Africa that their civil wars and severe troubles are the direct consequences of colonialism, exploitation and political interference by foreign governments.

പ

For all we know the recitation of what is ultimately, entirely, unbearable, but real and consequent, the litany of the atrocities of our own doing, is the means through which the holy invocation can be activated.

∽

A story. Going to the cave involved me in a deep story that will take years to understand. Going to Liberia was the same. We were involved in a story and we could not always determine whether we were involved in difficulty or blessings.

Because the roads were so muddy, and the country so poor, inevitably, one of the cars broke down on the way to Voinjama. Because the car broke down, some of us went on and Bill Saa and Tornorlah Varpilah stayed behind. Because we said we would send a car for them, they couldn't continue when their car was repaired. Because the roads were so bad we couldn't send a car until the morning. Because of this they stayed overnight in a small town half way to Voinjama. Because of this, a man who was also overnighting overheard their conversations about peacebuilding. Because the roads were so muddy, they reached several impasses during the journey of the next day. Because everyone suffers equally, the man's car was also mired in the mud. This happened several times. Because the roads were so muddy and everyone's car was mired, they had to help each other out of the impasse and so became companions. Each time they spoke to each other more and more openly. After some hours, the man revealed that he had been a general in the government army. He said his war name had been General Leopard. General Leopard, who later asked us to call him by his given name Mohammed, (afterwards he changed his name to Christian Bethelson) questioned Bill and Tornorlah about their work and then said he wanted to tell **everyday gandhis** his story. He spoke on camera of all the atrocities of war that he had participated in, and there was nothing that was awful that he had not participated in. "You know," he said, "we capture the young boys and we coerce them, we beat them, we terrify them and we drug them and make them kill their brothers or sisters or mothers or fathers. And then there is no one they cannot kill and they have no choice but to continue killing."

He said, "A soldier doesn't rape and kill and gut a pregnant woman because he is in lust. He does it because he is desperate and he needs her *mana*, her power, her spirit to fortify him."

"One day," he said, "I was sitting under a mango tree and I looked at my hands. What kind of man am I?" I asked myself. "What will I tell my children about who I have become and what I have done? Then I wanted to put war behind me forever."

Henrietta Sumo, whose own son had been killed in the war, rose up, walked to him with great dignity, took him in her arms and said, "You are forgiven, my son. Come home." She is one of the organizers of the Liberia Women Mass Action for Peace, a movement of grassroots women organized by the Women In Peacebuilding Network, WIPNET. These Liberian women ended the war by sitting in the streets in protest and taking back the guns from the combatants.

Photo of Henrietta Sumo
& General Leopard (Mohammed) "You are forgiven"
© 2006 by André Lambertson

From **RANTIFESTO**, by Cynthia Travis, March, 2006

How does one live to create and sustain miracles?

Ask the women of Liberia, who dreamed the 15-year civil war would happen before it came, then stepped into a miracle that stopped it.

Liberians divide their civil war into "World War 1," "World War 2," and "World War 3," in order of magnitude. During "World War 3," in early 2003, a small group of Muslim women active in peacebuilding wondered what they could do as women to end the war. Soon there was a core group of 12, from a mix of religious and tribal groups. Hoping to attract 20 or 30 more, they called a public meeting and 500 women showed up.

Every day from sunrise to sunset, with rockets and bullets flying overhead, they gathered on the side of the road, then in the road, sitting on the ground in searing sun and torrential rain. They refused to speak. They refused food and water. They began visiting rebel camps, listening to "their boys" and collecting guns. Within two months, Charles Taylor had fled ("I can no longer deny the women. If they want me to leave, I will go.") and a ceasefire had been called. Peace talks were convened in Ghana. Of the 75 delegates invited to attend, only one of the women was invited. So they took money that Charles Taylor had tried to bribe them with, and sent an additional 13 women to monitor the talks. Standing at the door of the hall, word came that the ceasefire was in jeopardy. So they locked the delegates inside and left the premises with the key. No food or water, no bathrooms, for the people inside. Needless to say, the ceasefire was signed. And now, three years later, democratic elections have been held and Ellen Johnson Sirleaf, modern Africa's first woman president, has been elected. Prominent peacebuilders and environmentalists are being appointed to government positions.

The Liberian women created a better reality by literally sitting in it. They followed classic Gandhian nonviolence strategies (without knowing that's what they were doing). They insisted on a miracle and it was so.

The women had suspended their vigil one time before when it seemed the war was over. One woman, however, was continuing the vigil next to the American embassy when a mortar shell exploded next to her killing several people but without injuring her. She was so stunned and grieved by the explosion that she couldn't move or speak until a man came to her to tell her that she was alive. Rousing, she walked more than five miles to the field where the women originally kept the vigil and sat down alone. Another woman saw her and joined her and then, as if by magic, the rest of the women gathered and the vigil was re-instated.

Mohammed said, "I want to work with you. I want to be an **everyday gandhi** too. I want to work with the child soldiers and bring them home from war."

On March 7, 2006 Cyndie Travis said that Mohammed is seeking out ex-combatants, many of whom are very young, virtually children, from the former rebel army who are training again in the Liberian forests for potential guerrilla warfare in Guinea. He speaks to them about the horrors of war and explores possibilities of other kinds of training and education so that they can find meaning and opportunity in civilian life.

All the time that we were in Africa, Cyndie had been longing to see a leopard in the wild. And now, in an unexpected form, she had met one.

જ્જ

When we came home, a Torah portion, Chapter 58 of Isaiah, part of the Yom Kippur reading, came in an email from Rabbi Arthur Waskow. Thinking that the portion "bears several strong hints at calling for the Jubilee," and the possibility that the Prophet had in mind "the release of indentured servants," Waskow fantasized "Isaiah elbowing his way thru the crowd at the Temple or through the crowd at a Super-Synagogue in Babylonia – and interrupting – shouting out [a] radical challenge to the liturgy." Unfortunately, the result of the Rabbis' assigning this to be read on Yom Kippur is that it becomes not a challenge to the liturgy but a part of it. There is a wonderful story by Franz Kafka:

"One day a leopard stalked into the synagogue, roaring and lashing his tail. Three weeks later, he had become part of the liturgy."

And now our Leopard also has become part of the liturgy.

"How do you say 'good-bye' in your people's language?" General Leopard asked Cyndie after learning she is Jewish.

"You say, *shalom*," she answered, "and it means peace."

Shalom, Salaam to Mohammed, our leopard who has joined **everyday gandhis** as a peacemaker.

જ્જ

On Rosh Hashanah, Cyndie Travis and I had been seated on a bench outside a crude shelter when the (too) young tribal chief, one of the few young men who had managed to survive the war, came toward us and said, smiling, "You are our strangers and we welcome you" and placing one of the toddler twins in Cyndie's arms, extended to us, the two white women, full, openhearted hospitality.

We were there because our cars were mired in the mud again as we were returning to Monrovia from Voinjama. Because we were stuck in the mud we had to stay overnight in the village and because we stayed overnight in the village, we came upon the Liberian women from WIPNET dancing, singing, praying for peace as they do every Monday at the roadside of each town and we prayed and sang and danced with them. Because of the successful elections, the women disbanded their mass action roadside demonstrations a few weeks later. We had been privileged to witness the last of these historic gatherings.

In the midst of a war-torn country, we were taken in by strangers who trusted us, fed us, though many of the people are hungry. In the midst of a war-torn country amidst rumors of the war beginning again and ex-combatants, former child-soldiers, some still virtually children, massing at the borders of neighboring countries, we were invited into a peacemaking process unlike any we knew even in our own country.

ↄ

This you must understand: In the midst of a war-torn world, in the midst of elephant exile, of virtual imprisonment in tiny and overcrowded preserves, the Ambassador who came first in 2000 and again in 2001 came five or six times in September of 2005.

We had gathered, as I said, a group of ambassadors of our own. We were from California, New York, Cape Town, the Kalahari and Liberia – peace builders, activists, shamans, filmmakers, visionaries – but also spiritually supported by people from everywhere on the globe. The Ambassador that we believed had called us there, came and met us. It was and remains entirely astonishing.

The great elephant herds of the Kruger National Park, under threat of culling, are migrating in growing numbers across the border into Mozambique's adjacent Limpopo Park. Flying by helicopter over Limpopo Park, we could see several herds and single bulls moving through the bush that had formerly been denuded of game by Mozambique's protracted war and by serving as a *coutada*, or hunting ground, under earlier Portuguese colonial rule.

Also on the helicopter flight, sponsored by South Africa's Peace Parks Foundation, was an excited Dr. Markus Hoftmeyr, head of Kruger's veterinary wildlife services.

He believes that the elephants are signaling each other, sometimes in sounds that carry far but are inaudible to the human ear, that it is safe to return to their old stomping grounds in the Mozambican area now that the war is over and it no longer serves as a hunting place or as a "bushmeat" abattoir for guerrilla fighters. This is a remarkable change from four years ago, when most of the first group of 25 elephants, who were symbolically handed over to Mozambique by former president Nelson Mandela to start repopulating their park, made a dash back to the safety of Kruger.

> Most found openings in the high-security fence at river cross-
> ings, but Hoftmeyr says one bull trundled for many kilometres along
> the fence until he was able to round it where it meets the Limpopo
> River border in the far north. http://www.peaceparks.org/

At the end of this essay or letter or cry, I will tell the story of the Am-
bassador(s) who came. It is not how it happened chronologically, but it is
in its way the last word and also the beginning.

After the Elephant Ambassador came the first time, Michael and I
and others initiated Daré inspired by the social intelligence of elephant
herds. Though many elephants have been driven mad as a consequence
of human behavior, left to themselves they are models of social cohesion.
Now, after this visitation, I see that I am/we are being called into a writing matrix. This book, for now, yes, I know it is a little book and not an
essay or a pamphlet, but a book, like *Entering the Ghost River*, is something
I did not imagine. Perhaps it is a matrix of knowledge that is among us,
becoming visible, of us, but not of us, like a dream. When I met the Ambassador the first time, Daré was a consequence. Now after this meeting ...
a matrix of vision ... a Daré of the written word.

> DARÉ QUESTIONS:
>
> How Do We Sustain Each Other?
>
> How Do We Heal Each Other?
>
> What Are We Being Called To Give?
>
> What Are We Being Called To Do?
>
> How Do We Serve Spirit?
>
> How Do We Live The Dharma?
>
> Principles of Daré
>
> Daré needs to be experienced and lived in order to be known.
> Still, there are certain principles that are fundamental to it.
>
> The strength and essence of Daré is in the circle and its intelli-
> gence. Council is its heart. And in Council one always speaks from
> the heart and allows the spirits and ancestors to speak through one.
> Wisdom comes from the combined voices and presence of every-
> one who is participating. The purpose of Council is to seek answers
> from the community that we can't find ourselves. Asking and ad-
> dressing a single question coheres the community.

Daré begins by calling in the spirits. Everything depends on this. The invocation allows Spirit to inform the participants. It creates a field of knowing and remembering. Daré also centers on telling dreams and receiving dreams as gifts from the ancestors to the circle. Council and dreams are channels between the world of the living and the world of the invisibles.

Music is another essential element. For thousands of years it has been the way that people have called Spirit and that Spirit has made itself manifest. In Daré, the voice and the drum as well as other instruments are essential components for invocation as well as healing.

Daré is for the sake of healing, but we don't presume to say we know what healing is, how it occurs, or even how, always, to recognize it. Sometimes one is the healer and sometimes one is desperate for healing. Sometimes the two activities are one in the moment. Healing is, thus, an interchange, the dynamic of giving and receiving.

In 2001, after September 11th, we began to devote the concern of the Topanga Daré to peace-making. Again, we don't know how peace-making proceeds, but we have determined to make it the center of Council. Sometimes the questions are direct: "Describe moments in your life when you have participated in or received the benefits of peace-making. What are the principles that were at the core of this experience?" And sometimes we address other questions in Daré, but always knowing that healing and peace-making are the ground of everything we do.

Everyone is welcome and welcomed in Daré. Everyone is listened to and heard without judgment. This generous mind is not easy to attain, it takes time, practice and dedication. Welcoming, praising and blessing are the core of it. Daré is the place where each person's individual genius, intelligence and particularity is sought out, acknowledged and called forth.

And finally, Daré is truly composed of all the members of the community, living and non-living, visible and invisible, the humans and the non-humans, the people, trees, birds, animals, stones and elementals. When all the beings gather, Daré comes to be.

These are some of the basic principles, but it isn't a checklist. Daré emerges when people gather, some familiar, some strangers, with the intention of manifesting in the moment a community in which such principles are vibrant and alive. Each gathering, then, is different as it responds to those who have come together, their joy and suffering, and as it responds, of course, to the circumstances of the times. When we leave each other, we are different because we have allowed ourselves to be altered and because we are carrying Daré mind into all our other relationships. But, all of this comes about because everyone who comes is deeply committed to and engaged in the ongoing process of exploring how such a way of being might come to be.

THE INSPIRATION FOR THE BLUE FLAG DARÉ

Augustine Mandaza Kandemwa, an indigenous Shona healer from Zimbabwe, introduced Michael and Deena to the idea of the Daré or Council. In Bulawayo, Zimbabwe's second largest city, Mandaza has re-imagined a tribal form in an urban setting. Daré is a healing community composed of all the members of the natural world where exchange is constant and dynamic. Mandaza believes that many diseases are caused by 'the heaviness of the gods upon us.' The healer acts on behalf of Spirit, calling people forth, opening the path between the individual and Spirit, removing the obstacles to the spiritual life. The ways of coming to Spirit are many and can be both arduous and beautiful. Song, prayer and ritual are as essential to the healing process as are medicine, treatment, dream interpretation, divination and service.

In the Shona and Ndebele traditions, the gods heal through us. "I am God's feet, I am God's hands," Mandaza likes to say. The healer's task is to create himself or herself into the vessel that can carry the healing spirit. In any given moment, the healing spirit passes through a room and anyone who has the capacity receives it on behalf of the community. Ultimately, there is no great distinction between the healer and the one who needs healing, just as the beggar can be the angel who calls forth our gifts and generosity, the one who is ill calls forth the healing spirits in the healer as the healer invokes them in the one who is ill. Through initiation one is both healed and empowered to bring healing to the community. The members of the community learn to heal each other; the one who receives is called forth to develop the capacity to return the gift. As the healer must be sustained in order to heal, the question the community poses to itself is: how can we sustain each other?

Healing is not a profession; it is a way of life. Exchange is not limited by money or one's ability and so the sacred and beautiful are not commoditized or commercialized. Such a Daré is based on the idea of the gift as a sacred responsibility. We are given gifts. These gifts are for the sake of the community. We add what we can to them. We pass them on. Such is the way of the authentic and meaningful life.

Poetry and Art are not professions; they are sacred activities and ways of life. A creative community is based on gifts as sacred responsibilities given to us for the sake of the community. We add what we can to them. We pass them on. Such is the way of the authentic and meaningful life.

At this terrible beginning of the 21st century, it is essential to re-imagine art, healing and community. These gatherings are seeds for beginnings we cannot yet conceptualize. The task is to see how we can each come forth to meet and ease each other's suffering and concerns.

No rules, protocols, minutes, legislation, organization, statements of purpose, tax deductions, agendas. But: meditation, Council, medicine, hands-on healing, conversation, shamanic work, curanderismo, divination, ritual, cooking, reading, gardening, prayer, poetry, dance, song, art, listening, silence, healing ....

We will bring what we have to offer and we will form and reform in the course of the day into what configurations develop. We will call each other forth, receive from each other in the ways we can and will offer to each other what we can. To receive what heals and to offer what sustains, this is the goal.

"I owned a small shop on the main street. Baba, the old healer, wanted to teach me secret songs and how to prepare medicines. He said I was an *ojha*. I prayed to the goddess for direction. She came upon me. "Close your shop and build a temple in this field. Fly a red flag from the roof. You will become an *ojha*. Do not worry about money or your family's needs. I closed my shop the next day and everything has come to be. I could not sing before and now I have a beautiful voice to heal with, a gift from the goddess!" Babaji — From Pat Moffit Cook, Shaman, Jhankri and Nelė, Music Healers of Indigenous Cultures.

The Beggar's Prayer: The world I love is in great need of healing and I am incapable of healing it. Please help me.

೧

I was a keynote speaker for the national meetings of the American Academy of Environmental Medicine in October, 2005 and spoke words that were insisted through me.

Afterwards, some of the physicians applauded and some said that I am mad. Yes, of course, I am/we are, indeed. Who that is sane would not be mad in such times? And who that pretends to be sane is not mad to do so?

What were some of the words of the madwoman?

"Some years ago the term 'post modernism' was formulated. It spoke of this epoch born out of the horrors of the 20th century. It included in its origins major events of the 20th century, WWI, the Holocaust and atomic bombs. Today such a time line would include World War I, mustard gas, aerial bombing of civilian populations, World War II, the holocaust, fire bombing of cities, nuclear attacks on Hiroshima and Nagasaki, Chernobyl§, Love Canal, Vietnam, chemical warfare, napalm, Agent Orange, land mines, depleted uranium, distinct and frequent acts of terrorism, Abu Ghraib, Guantanamo, global warming, toxic waste, pesticides, global pollution of earth, air and water, and global environmental degradation. These events describe a reality that no people ever in the history of the world have had to face, to which no one is immune; the situation is global, and life itself is threatened by those 'tipping points,' the polar ice melting and the Siberian peat bogs releasing methane gas....

"The normal round of birth, life and death is over and physicians are being asked to reassess the nature and practice of medicine in order to meet these times of catastrophe. The epidemics of cancer and autoimmune diseases are a consequence of a culture that is violent, toxic and disconnected from the natural order. The horrors we are creating are legion, rampant and may be irreversible. Language stutters to express this understanding because our cultures are not required to give words to such truths. We have entered the time of catastrophe....

"Wars do not end when the truces are signed. The effects of the war on the populations and on the earth are continuous. Cancer and war are not unrelated to each other and not only because we 'make war on cancer' as we 'make war on mosquitoes' but because the weapons we are developing continue to fire, assaulting citizens, soldiers, personnel, animals, everyone and every thing who was or continues to reside on that now toxic and radiant land....

"But the patients who are supported by the physicians in their knowledge that their diseases and injuries are caused by toxic waste, radiation poisoning, depleted uranium, Agent Orange, or the impossible stresses of war have a better chance of healing than those whose physicians enter into the denial endemic to government agencies, medical re-

---

§ *See* www.elenafilatova.com, *and the Appendix in this book by Stephan David Hewitt entitled "Chernobyl: Prometheus Unbound."*

...rchers, the media and the military....."

> Denying the effects of weaponry or technology is not a fault of Americans alone. This was certainly the case in Chernobyl. "When people insisted that their sickness and exhaustion, their cancers, miscarriages, and deformed babies, had something to do with Chernobyl, they were diagnosed with "radiophobia" an irrational fear of radiation."
>
> Joanna Macy [xxv]

"The most important patient that the physician must attend is the environment. We cannot hope for the human to recover if the environment is continually assaulted. What the earth suffers, the patient suffers and the physician does not escape being a patient."

✑

The arctic is melting. The polar bear cubs fail to thrive. They become hermaphrodites from toxins building up in their bodies. Many of the bears are dying of starvation; they cannot swim the sometimes 70 miles between ice floes and the land where they must hibernate. The white milk of the white polar bear against the receding snow is as dark with chemicals as are their lives. The great wild-hearted mother bear whirling in her grief is helpless against us. What is the practice that prepares us to allow God to speak through us on behalf of creation? Like Balaam, how might we be forced into blessing?

If it is possible to invite all the creatures of the world into a holy alliance on behalf of creation, we must do it.

> We must also recognize, as with my experience with the elephants, when we are ourselves being called into alliance by them. Shortly after I wrote these words about the polar bears, I had the following dream:
>
> *There are two black bears. The mother bear is in an area that is penned but not enclosed so she is wherever I am, in the house or in the partitioned area outdoors; we are not in the wild. The small bear with the pointy face and very sharp pointed teeth comes toward me and bites me on the thigh. The pain is very sharp. I do not flinch. I wait for the pain to subside and for the bear to see that I am calm and then gingerly and gently reach to pet her behind the*

ears the way I stroke my companion wolves Akasha and Blue. The mother is not concerned about me. The little bear begins to trust me. The kind of trust I have with the wolves develops.

In classic shamanism, a bite in a dream signifies the dreamer being called into a totemic alliance with the animal. I was aware of this while dreaming and that is why I was so careful to receive the cub rather than flinch or display fear. When I awakened, I was surprised that the bear was black and also puzzled by its features.

Research revealed it to be a Spirit bear, or Kermode bear, a black bear from the rain forests of British Columbia that carries recessive white genes and so is often white, hence the name, but is often black.

On March 1, 2006, it was announced that after years of disputes with logging companies, government, industry, environmental, and indigenous groups, British Columbia agreed last month to create a massive new wilderness preserve. The Great Bear Rainforest lies within a 15.5-million-acre region of steep-sided fjords and islands along the Canadian province's Pacific coast. Under the deal, the new park's 4.4 million acres (1.8 million hectares)—nearly twice as large as Yellowstone National Park—are off limits to loggers and largely closed to mining exploration. Logging companies can fell trees in a sustainable manner over the rest of the region.

"[The agreement is] a living process, which I don't think is ever finished. But in today's terms, I think we have balance," said Gordon Campbell, premier of British Columbia.

According to tribal legend, a godlike creator in the form of a raven turned one of every ten black bears white to remind humankind how clean the Earth was during the Ice Age.

I journeyed to the bear to see why I was being gifted by such a relationship, difficult as such an initiation might turn out to be. I was reminded of the classic myth of the bear retold in many places, but with particular insight and understanding in Paul Shepard and Barry Sander's *The Sacred Paw: The Bear in Nature and Myth and Literature* (with an Afterword by Gary Snyder, Arkana, Penguin, New York, 1992).

In the Haida version of the myth, one of the young girls out picking huckleberries is complaining instead of singing to warn the bears of her presence. This is an offense and a blasphemy and the bears carry her off to their home. There she lives with the Bear people, sees when they put on and take off their skins, and eventually marries the bear and has twins with him, half human, half bear.

Sometime later she sees her brothers searching for her and alerts them to her presence. "The Bear Husband knew that he must die, but before he was killed by the woman's brothers, he taught her and the Bear Sons the songs that the hunters must use over his dead body to ensure their good luck. The Bear sons removed their bear coats and became great hunters. They guided their kinsmen to bear dens ... and they instructed the people in singing the ritual songs. Many years later, when their mother died, they put on their coats again and went back to live with the Bear People."

Through the journey I understood that I was being reminded to practice the sacred songs and was also called to live with the Bear People. This does not literally mean to live in the bears' territory, though it may mean, in the shamanic sense, to take on a spirit spouse, which, as Barbara Tedlock frequently points out, is a classic requirement for diviners and shamans. This reinforces the teaching about making a primary alliance with the beings of the natural world. It is a reiteration of what I learned during my time in the cave. I was called to a unique but ancient alliance with nature at the beginning of the time covered by this essay and now again at the very end as I prepare this book for publication.

Sometimes we invite the animals into council and sometimes they come and take us where they want us to go. Carol Sheppard had such a dream on June 1, 2004. This became one of the dreams that has been guiding our community because it reminds us that we cannot look away.

I had a dream where I grew heavy, fatigued. I could feel the spirits wanting, calling me, pulling my own will away so my body would be theirs. I tried to lay myself down as the cloak of heaviness consumed me but fell onto the earth, limp and not in control of my body. I went under that fog and entered a dream within the dream, dreaming that I was dreaming.

A large ancient bird, a pterodactyl, entered my body. My bones and flesh stretched, creaking from the push of it inside me forcing my body into the shape and size that was necessary to hold it. It was unconcerned about my discomfort. And then, when it had taken my body as its own, it took flight. Out of the room, straight through the wall which had no solidity and up, up and high, wings beating, heart pumping. Its voice inside me shrieked the command, "Look down!

Look down!" I was consumed with trepidation and vertigo, did not want to shift my focus down but the pterodactyl's command would not, could not be ignored. I shifted my gaze just enough to look down. "What do you see? What do you see?" it fiercely demanded again. We were passing over a dense city made of stone, smoke stacks everywhere belching heat and soot, black thick smoke. I thought I could not bear it though I did not know why, for I was confused and didn't understand what I was being shown. The self whose body was being flown was caught in fear, confusion, vertigo, and the self with useless body lying on the earth struggled, paralyzed, to shake it loose, to come back. I lay in my own bed, aware of them both in a state of clear light lucid dreaming for some long moments. As I awoke the words "First Bird" were on my lips.

Carol had this dream a year before she moved to the land where Michael and I live. She could not have known that I had, some months before, journeyed to the spirits of this land in order to begin a process of making the land a sanctuary for all the creatures who live here, a sanctuary, first for the land itself. The spirit that came when I journeyed was pterodactyl and it called itself, First Bird. *(See page 23)*

(See page 23)

ℰℑ

I was blessed to be able to speak to the physicians. The entire globe, every extant society, every culture, every tribe, every nation, every single individual, every creature is in grave need of healing.

The talk to the AAEM had been contracted long before Katrina and Rita but was given afterwards. A physician I met in the coffee shop in the hotel told me he had left his wife, children and mother in Florida still, after a week, without electricity and without gasoline for the car. "No one knows what we are suffering," he said.

There was no mention of these catastrophes at the conference, when one would think they would speak about nothing else but these signs of further deterioration of the environment, the medical consequences and the fearful future. After all, Cancer Alley in Louisiana, with its toxic ooze was hard hit by Katrina. Cancer Alley is the site of petrochemical companies whose liquid horror emptied into the streets and into the waterways, combining with oil and gasoline to cake in mud or dissolve in Pontchartrain, the Mississippi, and the Gulf where it meets the rest of the flotsam and jetsam of the other hells we have created. *(See page 38.)*

Before she left Los Alamos, Alexis Lavine began studying Cranial Sacral Dynamics. The following is excerpted from her unpublished essay, "The Earth and Healing: Messages from the Wisdom of Cranial Sacral Dynamics, Geology and Spirit."

How can I apply ways of doing healing work with the body to doing healing work with the earth? ...What are some of the ways of knowing and working with the places that call for healing? ... I was called to the study of geology out of a desire to help teach people to respect the earth and its processes and to teach people to live in right relationship to the earth. I have also always been called to hands-on healing work with people. I never imagined the two being connected. ... Working at Los Alamos National Laboratory [was] a huge challenge and made me ask myself "How and where can I see the potential for health in the Lab?" The realization came that it lies within the people, the earth, the plants, and the animals and that my work was to call this forth while bringing light into the darkness. ...I've wondered in recent years why my life's journey brought me into places of extreme imbalance — this was answered by the words: "When things are not in balance, there's the highest potential to engage healing."

Just as trauma gets stuck in our bodies, so it can get stuck in the earth, (energy can be held in places that have experienced trauma.) Healing trauma can be engaged by examining the stories it is part of in our lives. Just as we carry our stories with us in who we are, how our energy moves, and how we relate to all around us, so earth carries its story. It holds not only the stories of trauma, but also the stories of beauty, the stories of the ancestors and their connections with the earth. I have been called to such a place, where the ancestors were in sacred union with and reverence of the earth. The ancestors have left messages of their ways in the earth to be uncovered at the right times. They have shown me the natural intelligence of the earth, and ways to offer healing.

೧

After the sojourn in the cave, I went with Alexis to the suffering land where nuclear waste and other chemicals from experiments at Los Alamos have been dumped into the canyons, and are carried by the waters.

Last year, the spirits led Alexis, then a geologist at Los Alamos, to find a cave on land that originally was a sacred home to the Tewa people and that we visited together in July 2005. (An identified sacred cave at Los Alamos has been closed with steel mesh and bars and is inaccessible even to the native people.)

This cave is a *sipapu*, a portal to the spirit world. We came in under a heavy cloud cover that arose suddenly. We had been required to change the time of our visit so many times, we had to accept that we were being called to this place at this exact moment. Though the sky had been clear, I had the premonition that we would encounter weather and soon we were accompanied by the rumble of thunder. Alexis stopped, advising me that the cave was around the bend and it was time for us to take off our shoes. As we did, lightning flashed closer and closer and then it thundered again and hail fell furiously.

We huddled momentarily under a tree that didn't protect us and then made our way barefoot over mounds of hail to another cave from which we watched the display of lightning and of hail dancing. Thunder continued to astonish us with its force and proximity. It was as if we were in it and we blessed the Thunder Beings for gifting us with their presence. Water was streaming through the adjoining cave, a small flash flood, that didn't enter where we were despite the hole at the level bottom of the common stone wall. After the storm, we made our way to the cave we were seeking. The only standing body of water we saw was in a small rock in front of the cave. Everything around us was renewed, vibrant and alive from the gift of the abundant water as if we were being given a sign about the possibilities of restoration.

Words were given to me to speak aloud to the spirits of the land: "Los Alamos is not forever. We have come to make an alliance with the spirits of the land. We do not know how to do this but we have come nevertheless. Alexis will invite those who practice the old ways, the people to whom this land belongs and from whom it was appropriated, to this place to resume as best as they can their ceremonies of purification and hope. We are searching, also spiritually, for the ways out of the disaster that is being created here every day. We are deeply sorry and we are willing to carry the grief."

Driving back to Alexis's house we reached the summit of a long hill just as the sun was setting. The setting sun was shining directly into my eyes and I had to pull over to the side of the road. The sunset was spectacular, a sea of radiant oranges and purples. We had been brought, again, to this place at this time, to witness beauty.

Gratitude and, again, hope.

ℰ⅋

I asked the physicians of the AAEM to listen to the talk as patients. One of the other speakers had announced that one in three men and one in two women will suffer cancer in their lifetime. Everyone in the room had had cancer or had cancer now or would have cancer or had family who had had or was suffering or would suffer cancer. Certain knowledge and understanding cannot come from outside the self:

"Before cancer, we are all humbled and vulnerable. Cancer emphasizes our mortality. Those physicians willing to enter the heart of sorrow with the patient stand a better chance of bringing healing with them than those who hide behind clinical detachment. Cancer, if we meet it with the patient's mind, teaches us compassion and compassion offers us deep teachings and spiritual power with which we may meet the current crises and catastrophes.

"The root cause of any injury or illness is not irrelevant – it changes the nature of the condition and so, among other responses, its treatment. The technology of amputating a leg may be the same for a freak accident or one that is a consequence of war or a natural disaster that is no longer really natural. The same procedures may be followed in the operating room, if there is an operating room, but everything is different. If it is acknowledged that the patient's cancer is caused by Agent Orange, or other war related tragedies, or that the suffering is the inevitable consequence of participation in an unjust and illegal war, the patient responds differently to the illness and healing becomes possible."

"I am walking through Ward 57, the amputee ward, walking on the 5th floor. There are grisly sights here. Sights that the dining room and outside benches do not want to see, that I do not want to see. Bodies wrapped in blood soaked bandages. Eyes covered in agony. Nurses huddled over broken bodies. The air is thick on the 5th floor, hard to breathe... I feel a deep anger at America rising in me... At Walter Reed, ground zero for ugly war, there is no break from horror. A young man sits down on the bench next to me - 'blew the lower part of my leg off. .. an IED (Improvised Explosive Device)... getting my first leg next week... getting my first leg next week....

"Whether the 'For What?' is answered with a closed mind or with an honest answer, many seriously disabled veterans will in time turn bitter and cynical. But others will swallow hard, refusing to let the injustice crush them, and move on in life. But all will be deeply scarred. If their sacrifices were truly for the defense of our country, that helps a lot. That cause can justify the sacrifices but an unworthy cause justifies nothing. Americans are barely paying attention... a clear indication this is not a war for the defense of America. We have an administration that won't fully fund veteran's health care while it does not properly equip our troops in a war.... This is wrong America. Wrong to those with "road kill" legs, wrong to those with partial faces, wrong to those with missing limbs."

— Stewart Nusbaumer, "The Costs of War at Walter Reed," *Intervention Magazine.* http://www.interventionmag.com/

What I couldn't say at the outset but implied within the body of the talk was that most of the cancers we were suffering – as well as global catastrophes – are of our own making. The result of toxins and medicine and war, we will suffer the consequences for millennia.

❧

Just after our return from Liberia and before the talk at the AAEM, Ed Tick[§] joined the Topanga Daré for a council on dreaming for the world. Having re-introduced the old Greek forms of Asclepian dream healing, Ed also accompanies veterans and other victims of war back to Vietnam to en-

---

[§] *Regarding Ed Tick, See* http://www.mentorthesoul.com

gage in true healing work and restitution. Post Traumatic Stress Disorder can be healed, he asserts, in the sacred heart of the sacred interaction between the returning veteran and the Vietnamese he/she had once been trained to torture and kill. The legacy we have left in Vietnam is the horror of the consequences of Agent Orange but in Vietnam, as in the U.S., the consequences of Agent Orange are undocumented or denied. Despite their suffering and the devastation of the land, the Vietnamese receive Americans and veterans as friends. For the Vietnamese, Ed said, a war is entirely over when it is over. They expect forgiveness and friendship to follow directly. Thus they do not suffer PTSD as our soldiers do and they are able to reconcile and bring healing to those who *were* their enemy.

According to the BBC, 2/04,Vietnamese victims filed their first lawsuit against U.S. companies that produced the toxic defoliant used by American forces during the Vietnam War. The Vietnam Association for Victims of Agent Orange submitted the suit on behalf of two women and a man to a U.S. federal court. American veterans exposed to the herbicide, known as Agent Orange, had complained for years about health problems — cancer, diabetes and spina bifida — and sued some of the makers. That group says about three million people suffer from side effects. The U.S. Government says there is no direct evidence linking dioxin with the illnesses, but about 10,000 Vietnam War veterans in the U.S. allegedly receive disability benefits related to Agent Orange exposure. All three plaintiffs had worked in areas sprayed with Agent Orange. One female plaintiff suffered four miscarriages while the other has breast cancer. The man also has cancer and has two children with birth defects, the news agency reported.

"I do not want to do this for myself as it has been a long time already," said Phan Thi Phi Phi. "But in Vietnam, the poorest, the most miserable and the most discriminated ones are the Agent Orange victims so anything I can do for them, I will." At least 10 U.S. companies are named in the suit.

Published on Tuesday, March 28, 2006 by Reuters

Agent Orange Victims Gather to Seek Justice

HANOI - Vietnam War veterans from the United States, South Korea, Australia and Vietnam gathered on Tuesday to call for more help for the victims of the Agent Orange defoliant used by the U.S. military. Deformed children born to parents Vietnam believes were affected by the estimated 20 million gallons of herbicides, including Agent Orange, poured on the country were brought to the conference as dramatic evidence of its effects. "The use of Agent Orange in Vietnam produced unacceptable threats to life, violated international law and created a toxic wasteland that continued to kill and injure civilian populations long after the war was over," said Joan Duffy from Pennsylvania. Duffy, who served in a U.S. military hospital in Vietnam in 1969-1970, said the Agent Orange used there was more toxic than usual. "In an effort to work faster and increase production of Agent Orange, the chemical companies paid little attention to quality control issues," she said. "The Agent Orange destined for Vietnam became much more highly contaminated with dioxin as the result of sloppy, hasty manufacturing," she told the conference in Hanoi. Last March, a federal court dismissed a suit on behalf of millions of Vietnamese who charged the United States committed war crimes by its use of Agent Orange, which contains dioxin, to deny communist troops ground cover. The Vietnam Association for Victims of Agent Orange/Dioxin (VAVA) has filed an appeal, saying assistance was needed urgently as many were dying.

Dioxin can cause cancer, deformities and organ dysfunction. Manufacturers named in the suit included Dow Chemical Co. and Monsanto Co. VAVA chairman Dang Vu Hiep said Vietnam's lawsuit against U.S. chemical manufacturers was meant not only to help Vietnamese victims, but also victims in other countries. In January, a South Korean appeals court ordered Dow Chemical Co. and Monsanto Co. to pay $65 million in damages to 20,000 of the country's Vietnam War veterans for exposure to defoliants such as Agent Orange.

Ɒ

I must stop here. Pause here with me so that we can consider, together, what we have to consider, what we must look at, what we must see. When I began this book, I didn't know what it would consider. I didn't know it fully until today. What day is it? It is May 25, 2006. A book such as this is written in circles because any given moment or story contains the future – if we are fortunate. The moment there will be a moment without a future, it will be time to stop writing.

I have been stopped many times while writing this book. One of the first times I was stopped was when I read Ed Tick's essay, "From Dust to Gems: Agent Orange in Viet Nam Today."

"Yet the Vietnamese are not as plagued by the impact Agent Orange has had on their land as they are by its ongoing impact on their people, from the time of war until the present day. Agent Orange is water-soluble. Viet Nam's heavy rains have washed much of the defoliant through the ecosystem and out to the sea. But according to the Food and Drug Administration, its deadly poison dioxin is 100,000 times more potent than thalidomide as a cause of birth defects. It lodges in human and animal DNA, having tragic and disastrous effects down the generations. We do not know when, or if, it can ever be cleansed...

"Farther up the coast, in the ancient imperial capital of Hue, famous for the brutal battle for the citadel documented in the movie "Full Metal Jacket," Tu Ai, a woman in her twenties, tells her neighbor's story. The father of this family served in the war and was infected by Agent Orange. When peace came, he married and had seven children, all of whom were "strong, intelligent, and attending school." Each child, upon reaching the mid-teens, "became foolish." Their minds seemed to not only stop maturing, but to regress and decay. They lost their abilities to read, speak, even carry on everyday functions, until every one of the seven became completely helpless. The aging, heartbroken parents had to keep them in wooden cages while they desperately struggled to earn a subsistence living and seek some way to 'repair' their children."

I relegated the article entirely to the footnotes and had no intention of referencing photographs[§] that verify Ed's commentary, but what I have had to bear witness to today has made it impossible to do so. Today, this morning, someone sent me photos of starving children with the injunction not to look away, because in cutting and pasting the photographs he couldn't look away. And so he asked that everyone who received the photo share his witnessing. I couldn't deny him this. Or rather, I couldn't deny the children. I do not include the photos here because we are carrying so much but they are in the field and we all know

§ *"The Children of Agent Orange" by Dutch photographer Jan Banning.* http://www.photo.nl/Index20.html. *Ed's article originally appeared in* Utne Reader, *Jan/Feb 2005.*

now that we will be called to view them, also, one day.

And so I pause again. Stephan Hewitt and I have been speaking about Chernobyl; he writes about it in the Appendix to this book. "You have seen, haven't you," he asked me, "the photographs of the children of Chernobyl by Paul Fusco?"[§] I say I haven't. And so he sent me to the website below as I am sending you. The photographs are unbearable and as we are in danger, in this country, of causing such horror, we must look hard at them.

For many years I have been writing about the Bomb. Calling the Bomb and the Holocaust the two koans of the 20th century. And I have reminded people, again and again, that we were the ones who dropped the Bomb. But we have gone beyond this. Look at the photographs and read the texts. We must understand that we have done this and that these children, who were not the direct victims of war as are the children of Agent Orange, are still heirs of the research begun with the Manhattan Project at Los Alamos. And still the call for more nuclear plants and still the threat to bomb the Iranian nuclear facilities and still even James Lovelock whose book, The *Revenge of Gaia* inspired or provoked this book, calls for nuclear energy to replace oil. We can proceed with the plans to retain our ways of life only if we do not look at the consequences of our actions, if we do not see that we are doing this. Who are we? We are the ones who are causing this. Chernobyl was not the result of military operations. Only if we look hard do we have the possibility of gaining vision.

"I have participated in some of the International Atomic Energy Agencies' analysis on Chernobyl and the attempt to spin the health results.... Some of you may know that I was a commissioner on a low-level radioactive waste facility for the Midwest. Because of that experience I had opportunities to weigh in on what standards should be for both international and domestic events such as decommissioning nuclear power plants, terrorist acts, etc. The U.S. is aggressively trying to change the standards because they have so many nuclear facilities — from the national labs that were part of the Manhattan project to all the little nuke messes created by our health care and research systems to the mid-size debacles like the 13 nuclear power plants in Illinois. – From a letter to Deena from Carolyn Raffensperger, April 2006

§ http://todayspictures.slate.com/inmotion/essay_chernobyl

❧

I felt it was essential for the physicians at the AAEM to consider the relationship between individual illness and war:

"Cancer asks us to consider not only the particular illnesses, their possible causes and cures and treatments, but the mind, the global mind that has and continues to research and develop devilish poisons and toxins that last thousands of years. Cancer demands that we investigate what in ourselves and in our associates allows us to engage in such activities that have thrown the entire world into such crises.

"When John Wilson, MD, the AAEM conference convener and I were discussing the conference, he wrote … 'An important part of the environment is the emotional environment, especially fear, not only for individuals who hear the "C" word but also for society and the fear that pervades social consciousness about cancer.'

"The answer that came to me was simple: Cancer is a precise indicator on every level of our being that something is terribly wrong. Something is terribly wrong both in ourselves and in the world. We are a microcosm of grave disorder. We have been altered. The knowledge that a cell in us is no longer of us, is no longer functional, is no longer itself, that we have a mutant inside us, is terrifying. What has it become? What will we become?

"The suffering from the treatment for cancer has become commonplace even as cancer has become commonplace. Even as multiple cancers are becoming commonplace. What has become of our culture and our earth?

"Here is the place of our great fear and our great suffering. Cancer as event and metaphor speaks to us of environmental devastation. It speaks to us of rampant and unrestrained growth. It speaks to us of the takeover of the body by aberrant cells, particularly in its inability or unwillingness to be a functioning member of the body community, it speaks to us of damage so severe that only excision or death can save the system it has invaded. It speaks to us of the extremity of the irreversible damage to the environment that is ourselves and in which we live.

"The cancer cell is an entity on the front line. It is a wounded self that cannot be restored without thinking about healing in entirely new ways. It is the first victim of environmental disaster."

At the AAEM, I was privileged to be able to pose this question:

"What is the nature of the world we are living in and what are we being called to as healers and as physicians to meet it?"

౿౭

A series of "coincidences" very recently invited a conversation on email between Cyndie Travis, Nancy Myers, Lawrie Hartt, Bill Saa and others. I had come upon a reference to WIPNET, the non-violent action organization of women, sitting on the side of the road for peace, sitting there every day in the torrential rains and merciless heat that characterize Liberia's equatorial climate. At the point of peacemaking, the women who had brought down the government and the war with their relentless presence were told to go home and take care of the kitchen and the children. But they did not.

In an email, Cyndie Travis asked:

"The Liberian women were convinced that all was lost, but they didn't accept this. I began to wonder: What would the Liberian women do if they were convinced that the world was coming to an end?"

In the March/April 2006 issue of the **everyday gandhis** newsletter, Cyndie wrote: "The Liberian women who stopped the civil war did so by insisting on a miracle. What if the women of Liberia insisted on the restoration of sacred forests and waters? What if the world's environmental scientists began acting like the women of Liberia? What if we all did?"

౿౭

One gives a talk. One talks calmly and rationally. Smiles. Tries to make a joke. Reads a poem. But, actually, while I was speaking to the physicians, I was wailing inside. I was thinking of the ways conventional medicine tortures patients, the ways in which conventional medicine has constructed a hell simply by privileging its procedures, routines, tests and remedies no matter what the side effects or consequences may be.

A friend who is taking tamoxifen has opted for a hysterectomy to save herself the possibility of uterine cancer. As a young healer-counselor, I was undone when a client of mine whom I had seen through stomach cancer died of adhesions caused by radiation when, against her better judgment, she acquiesced to another round as a precaution. These medical treatments are not the skillful application of the precautionary principle but rather its opposite. "First do no harm" is no more the essential principle of modern medicine than it is a guiding principle of science.

Wingspread Statement on the Precautionary Principle, Jan. 1998.

Science and Environmental Health Network: "When an activity raises threats of harm to human health or the environment, precautionary measures should be taken even if some cause and effect relationships are not fully established scientifically. In this context the proponent of an activity, rather than the public, should bear the burden of proof. The process of applying the precautionary principle must be open, informed and democratic and must include potentially affected parties. It must also involve an examination of the full range of alternatives, including no action."
http://www.sehn.org/precaution.html

ଓ

In January it was revealed that Bayer, with its infamous history of collusion with Nazi doctors experimenting on concentration camp inmates, paid poor students in Heriot-Watt University, Edinburgh, 450 pounds each to drink pesticides that kill pests, bugs, weeds and rodents. Recently it was leaked that the Bush Administration promoted pesticide experimentation upon humans including pregnant women, children and infants.

Lauren Zack first alerted me to the administration's persistence in experimenting on the poor and the helpless. In December we offered her a Music Daré (a community sound and energy music healing ritual) because she is suffering environmental illness. The physicians and health practitioners and Daré members who had gathered for a week to enter into the practice of transforming from medical people to medicine people, met with Lauren for several hours before the ritual healing event. During the week, unknown to each other, several people, including one physician and Lauren herself, dreamed that they were prevented by the medical staff from taking care of their just born infants. Lauren also recounted spending hours as a child playing with the paints, most now declared illegal, her father had developed for a chemical company. At the end of what we call "Indigenous Grand Rounds," Lauren understood that as part of the regime of bringing healing to herself, she was to recognize the reality of Spirit that she, until then, found too frightening to admit. Accordingly, she now would focus on the beauty and healing possibilities she saw, searching for these as relentlessly as she had concentrated upon unearthing and alerting us to assaults against the earth. We have been gratified to see her health improve as a consequence.

A Medical Mentoring Week with Deena Metzger

An Invitation To Medical Doctors, Osteopaths, Chiropractors, Nurses And Other Health Practitioners To Enter Into Dialogue And Re-Visioning The Medical Professions For The Sake Of The World

When I gave the keynote speech at the national meetings of the American Holistic Medical Association in 2004, and again in speaking to the American Academy of Environmental Medicine in 2005, I asked essential questions: How does one transform from being a medical doctor to being a medicine person? How can medical doctors expand their visions and skills so that they carry medicine in the ways of healers? Another way of asking this is: How does a medical practice become a spiritual practice?

I have been addressing questions of medicine and healing for almost thirty years. Those who have been called to heal the bodies and souls of individuals are also being called to imagine the ways of healing the bodies and souls of our communities and the world itself. I am honored to be part of the call to revision medicine as an aspect of the critical task of re-visioning our culture so that the world moves toward healing instead of devastation.

Many physicians are no longer practicing conventional medicine, or are entirely disheartened, or are carrying a vision they don't know how to enact. At the same time, there is a deep sense of possibility and hope that comes from imagining a re-alliance between healing and medicine, imagining the soul of medicine restored.

I believe we are being asked to step into a new paradigm or, perhaps to re-enter an old paradigm of healing. Accordingly, this is an invitation to begin a process of initiation, mentoring, education, exploration and re-visioning, deepening the way of the healer for oneself and for others. It is an invitation to begin the process of becoming a medicine person participating in the cultural changes that seem to be mandated by Spirit.

☙

My beloved friend, teacher, analyst, father, brother, companion, elder, advisor to two U.S. presidents, and initiator of worldwide humanitarian reforms including, with others negotiating the elimination of corporal punishment in the armed services worldwide, John Seeley, one of the most compassionate, wisest, most developed men on the planet was "incarcerated" for forty days at one of the best hospitals in Los Angeles even though it was becoming clear that the hospital stay was contributing to his debilitation. Almost weeping, he said, "I cannot find my heart or my life here and I do not believe it is worth it to sustain this body if I cannot find myself."

᪉

Illness is a mystery. Illness is a path and a vision. Sometimes it takes us on a soul journey. The danger is that the hospital committed to our health may entirely eradicate the opportunity for the individual to do the inner work that illness is designed to instigate. At 93, soul work is the only meaning of John Seeley's illness. Soul work is what the hospital environment prevents.

᪉

A Dream, May 2005:

I am teaching Nancy Meyers how to pray. At first it is four-pointed prayer, four diamonds in four-pointed relationship to each other, a mandala. This is about healing.§ It is very simple and very exact. Then we are in a circle and I am teaching prayer in the circle. We do this together. One gives oneself entirely. Then a man is taken by the holy. He begins to dance, raising one hand and twirling around, not unlike a Sufi dancer but that he is not dancing a pattern, he is being danced. Then he is compelled to go outside. I raise my hand also as I do when I rattle and I begin to follow him. At first, it is to show respect to him before the others who are skeptical and wary. I see that he is being taken; as a teacher, I must honor him. There is a moment when we must decide whether it is a genuine communication that is coming to him or whether it is his personal and private intoxication. He is telling us that the Divine is going to come. This has been revealed to him. There is no reason not to follow him. I know that it is up to me to follow and I will no matter what the others do. The quiet decorum of the prayer circle has been broken. We go outside – we are in a desert-like landscape with dunes. If one looks in another direction, one sees that there is an area that approximates a road, a swath in the land though there is and is not anything to distinguish it from the rest of the landscape and some distance toward the horizon someone has hung a light or pointed globe as if a star hanging from the sky, a confirmation

---

§ *The focus of the prayer circle is the same person who is the subject of the poem at the end of this essay, "Pelicans in the Midwest."*

of the vision. It has become clear that this is not about him as the carrier of the vision but about what may occur. He was following as I was following. Here we are in the desert. Among sand dunes.

At this moment, the wind comes up. I know this vision was true and this is why we have come to this place in the desert. I lie down on the sand, full prostration. It is not a self-conscious act. There are others who are standing in front of me and I am afraid they will shield me from the wind that is the Divine. But they do not. Nothing can shield one from the wind, from the Divine. To my left, there are two men in a building that we can see into as if there is no wall between us. They seem crude and rough and are watching TV. They are in the contrived world of television while we are praying, learning to pray, taken by a vision, going out to meet the vision, prostrate before the coming of the Divine.

When I speak to Nancy, she says that the dream dune landscape resembles the area where she lives. The next day while speaking about the dream to Valerie Wolf as we buy coffee on the way to the ocean to pray on behalf of the earth, I spot a photograph on the front page of the *Los Angeles Times* of Crescent Moon Lake set among the dunes in the Gobi Desert. It has always been fed by underground streams but is now drying up due to global warming. The image is exactly the image from my dream, complete with a single building. If the lake were entirely missing from the news article instead of diminishing, we would have been standing in the middle of the lake in my dream. http://www.travelchinaguide.com/attraction/gansu/dunhuang/moon_lake.htm.

What might be the meaning of such synchronicities gathered together by the dream?

Sometimes the synchronicities enhance the content. But, often, as may be the case here, they verify for those of us who are trying to understand the nature of the world as events, external and internal, tangible and spiritual are presenting it to us, the mysterious fact of our interconnection and the weavings that the dreams and visionary events manifest. Over time we see the validity of other ways of knowing based on the story weavings of events, dreams and visions in our own lives. However, another level of connectedness is attained when the circumstances of our distinct lives are woven into yet other stories that involve others. The focus upon the individual yields to the wonder of interconnectedness.

From a letter to Nancy Myers and Carolyn Raffensperger of Science
and Environmental Health Network:

> Sitting alongside John Seeley at this time of his life that
> may be his crossing over, I am aware, sadly, that his religious
> life isn't holding him, in part because his Episcopal church of
> 25 years will not take a stand against torture ... And, for what-
> ever intrapsychic reason, he can't, being so depleted by illness,
> find the Divine on his own unless someone sings the old hymns
> to him. But, when I ask him to recount his life and point out
> the miracles in it, he can acknowledge them without having to
> believe scripture or me because the evidence is there in his own
> life. Rejuvenated by the presence of the Divine, he does not
> feel abandoned, but is willing to see what this difficult time
> might mean.

e⁄ɔ

No one escapes illness. No one escapes death. John, no matter his
graces, will not escape the common human jeopardy and the common
round of suffering. But we hope he and others will escape the pain and
suffering that are caused by the cultural forms and artifacts we have created. The pain and suffering that are not ours by nature or by fate. And
that we may find the forms that are the real hope in such a time.

e⁄ɔ

As many new thinkers are calling us to see the interrelationship of
all beings, to see the network of all life, it is just as essential for us to see
the inter-connected consequences of acts of destruction and devastation.
Ecology demonstrates the interconnections between life forms. An attack on any part of the web destroys the web.

Holistic medicine does not refer only to the range of healing methods integrated for the sake of patient care but also to the depth and range
of concerns that are involved in the causes, manifestation and treatment
of the illness as it appears in an individual and in the society. Compassion and truth telling are necessary components of medicine.

How have we been inadvertently absorbed into ways of thinking
that lead to cancer alleys, dead seas, killing fields, global warming, the
deaths of species and the natural world?

Walking the Creek

Waters from the snowy, sacred mountain,
Place of perfect balance, say the Chumash,
Once seeped down into the creek all year, cold
Even in August's fire season,
And then afterwards, into September
Even until the first rains of thanksgiving,
A trickle of the old stream, flowed.

Walking the creek this July morning
Gray river stones mark the graves
Of reeds alongside corpses of trees,
The brown dust of dry leaves,
This year's season, amber on the ground
Where we have known loam.

I dreamed Fire came in all her raiment
Over the ridge, and a petitioner
Took his drum and began praying
As if on his knees,
Praise to the Great One, as She descended
Among the torches of great oaks
And the fireworks of pines.

Fire is a god,
The hidden one, her power
Contained in stars,
The nuclei of strange particles and
The sacred magma at the core of planet earth.
We cannot drink it,
We must not take it in our hands.
    It does not serve us
    To breathe it in.

        Michael, the Archangel, Water
        And Gabriel, the Archangel, Fire,
        Together they are peacemakers,
        Who form heaven, *Sh'mayim*,
        Through the gathering
        Of the holy letters,
        Shin, the eternal flame
        At the core of fire, *Esh*,
        And *Mem*, the essence
        Of the sacred water, *Mayim*,

Sh'mayim, heaven,
Includes *Yud*, the Divine itself
And *Aleph*, the silent one,
At the beginning of beginnings,
Ever present in the word.

Fire season, we call it,
Not knowing, not wanting to know
the Holy One. Instead we make
A furnace of our world,
Separating the sacred from the sacred,
Water from fire,
Splitting the atom of paradise,
Fulfilling the prophecy of ultimate sin
Written this century
in the burning bodies of the holocausts
And the oldest ancestor's oily bodies.
The world is no longer
The Temple of the Sacred:
     It would be a sacrilege to call for Rain.
     Yes, it is a sacrilege to call for Rain.

July, 2006

A journal entry from a psychiatrist at a veteran's hospital:

"Then in the mid afternoon I 'processed' one of the most articulate PTSD sufferers I've come across. Just two days back from Iraq. Oh what pain. He told me such stories, painting word pictures of the burned bodies, the chunks and pieces of flesh after a car bomb, the random mortars, the filthy air heavy with diesel smoke and sand, the stinging flies, the odors, the children trying to sell their bodies, having to straighten twisted corpses to wrap them, his growing sense of rage and helplessness…. Too intense! My body rushed alternately cold and hot, my hair rose up in prickly shivers, I was nauseated. Sometimes being an intuitive and open to people's suffering is overwhelming to me. I wish I were more guarded. Or maybe not. Perhaps that is my gift, a powerful tool that can be a blessing to me, or a weapon that inadvertently harms. I expect I shall see one or two of his visions in my sleep tonight."

৶৶

An email reveals that someone in our kinship network has just been diagnosed with a virulent cancer that has metastasized. She has received a death sentence. Is her sentence different from the one that we have all received from the diagnostician James Lovelock? The Navajo separate the diagnostician from the one who offers treatment. The "treatment," in addition to gathering the community for a Sing is most often exact instructions on changing one's life and making amends for one's actions against individuals, the earth and the gods. As I write this, I think that we must offer her a Music Daré – our equivalent of the Navajo Sing.

I do not know what this person is called to do on behalf of her life and soul, but it is clear that as a species we are offending each other, the earth and the gods on a daily basis. The physician's fate is the same as the fate of any patient and the fate of any individual is exactly the same as the fate of the earth.

৶৶

Because of fourteen years of civil war, there is no remaining infrastructure in Liberia – no sanitation, no running water in many places, no electricity except by generator, no public transport, gasoline is sold in glass jars on street corners, and there is little food. In our travels south, we came upon a boy who had been driven 200 miles over impassable roads, the mud three to four feet deep, to get treatment for a broken leg only to be returning to the place he started from, untreated. We were told there are no physicians in all of Liberia except those associated with the UN who can only rarely be convinced to provide medical care and then only in emergencies. Because of the fundamental disruption of the society, the old ways practiced by traditional healers that bound the society together despite religious and tribal differences, are undermined as well. We did not know where he could find a doctor, a bone-setting *zo* or a medicine person. I was in the act of climbing into the truck to put my hands on him when our vehicle was freed from the mud and we had to go on but I was able to hand him some codeine for the rest of his journey. Under such dire circumstances, one longs to be of use and, also, in a harsh world, our concern may be the medicine he receives.

During a dream matrix-peacebuilding Council sponsored by the Topanga Daré and **everyday gandhis**, Danelia Wild had the following insight about Liberia, based on our understanding of sacred illness. Illness has the capacity to break someone down for the sake of initiation and transformation.

Thoughts on the Initiation of a Country

"Initiation is a story with a future. It is a process that that strips away old ways of being, removing obstacles between the soul and what it is being called to by Spirit. And it requires a shift in consciousness about what one is being called to — the path that is opening before one. Liberia finds itself stripped down — its physical infrastructure devastated along with its assumptions about the nature of kinship and community.

"And in this place everything now carries the creative possibility of conscious choice. Conscious choices that can be made on behalf of all creation — the land, animals, the people, the ancestors and spirits — all the participants in a living matrix of an initiated community.

"And so there are the questions, not merely of replacing what has been lost but of creating what is being called for by Spirit and the Ancestors. What kind of "re-building" serves this conscious creation of community? What kind of relationships are asking to be born? What kind of medical system? What kind of roads? What kind of education? How can the soul of the larger community that is this nation be served?"

To explore the area of sacred illness, see Deena Metzger, *Entering the Ghost River: Meditations on the Theory and Practice of Healing,* Hand to Hand; *Sacred Illness/ Sacred Medicine*, Michael Ortiz Hill and Deena Metzger, Elik Press; *Meeting Sacred Illness*, Michael Ortiz Hill and Deena Metzger, Elik Press.

One of the projects of **everyday gandhis**, in addition to documenting unique grassroots peace building efforts, is to revive the traditional mourning feasts on a national level. These feasts serve to help cross the spirits of the dead to their resting place on the other side of the river. Implicit to the ritual is the reconciliation of everyone who participates and mourns in order to eat out of a common bowl. In providing the means for the ritual – a cow for example able to feed an entire village – and in reviving the ritual itself, the medicine of social coherence is invoked. In the first ritual, former enemies, traditional people from the Lorma tribe and Mandingo people who follow Islam, mourned side by side. This having been accomplished, the elders were now able to reinstate their own rituals of purification that allow ex-combatants to return to the villages and be forgiven even for the atrocities that so many were compelled to commit against family and neighbors. The soldier-victims were tortured and soon they tortured. In order for the country to revive, the killers on all sides have to be reintegrated into the society. Healing comes in many different forms.

My Heart Does Not Call For Food: From Heartbreak To Hope in Liberia

By Cynthia Travis, **everyday gandhis** Founder & President

Journey to Lofa: First Reflections

In Liberia's civil war, over 1 million people were displaced and between 350,000 and 500,000 lost their lives. Most were never buried or mourned. In pre-war Liberia (and in most West African cultures) whenever someone died the entire community gathered to hold traditional mourning and feasting ceremonies as a way of sending their dear ones "across the river" to the ancestors. All sixteen tribes in Liberia practiced this tradition, holding the belief that there is life after death and that conflicts properly resolved at these gatherings permanently leave the community and are put to rest with the dead.

Until now, we at **everyday gandhis** have been focused on witnessing and recording stories of peacebuilding in the words of those that have known violence and war. The understanding that we were being called to revive Liberia's traditional mourning feasts was a surprise and came in a surprising way, growing out of two dreams. On the eve of my first trip to Liberia in 2004, the first dream came: *Bill and I and another colleague go at twilight to see Roosevelt (a friend living in a refugee camp in Ghana). We are standing on a cement landing next to a small river. Roosevelt is on the other side, holding a shaft of gray light like a staff. Beside him are three boxes that become three coffins that become three small wooden boats. He tells us, "Everything is ready." Behind him are twin towers in the style of the Tarot "Tower" card.*

The second dream: *I am on the battlefield at Gallipoli. I am walking among the bodies. All around me, men are wounded and dying. A circle of women forms around the battlefield, then each woman kneels by the body of a soldier, a husband, son or brother, and gathers his lifeless body into her arms. The women begin to weep and keen. The wailing becomes a song of piercing, terrible beauty.*

Traditional Liberian and African culture, like many indigenous wisdom ways, understands that dreams often come to individuals on behalf of the community, carrying specific guidance and infor-mation. Liberian researchers seeking to understand the genesis of their civil war discovered that many traditional women in the coun-tryside had dreamed the war would come before it happened: Dark clouds hovered over the countryside, raining blood. Blood ran in the streets like a river. A light-skinned dictator would rule the coun-try for 13 years.

Dreams are a way for the spirits, the animals and the ancestors to be in conversation with humans. They are a catalyst for events that 'want to happen'. ... In this case, the mourning feasts and tra-ditional ceremonies 'wanted' to happen.

In response to the complexity of what was unfolding both in Liberia and in our international 'dream circle', Bill and I spent months in meetings, correspondence and silent retreats. As we al-lowed the silence to envelop us, the wisdom of the dream images began to take shape as conscious possibilities. We began asking Liberian colleagues whether mourning feasts would be feasible, and whether people would want them, and learned that this had been under discussion for many months but for several reasons it had not been possible for the ceremonies to happen. ...How was it that we were drawn to serve in this way?

If we see the dreams as the catalyst, then what was favored was literally the bringing together of the community in a sacred way that allowed them to resume a lost dialogue with the ancestors, thus lifting a burden and source of discord from people's hearts.

Traveling to the northern province of Voinjama, we passed through the Firestone rubber plantations where, it is agreed, the workers live and work in slave conditions and the stench from the processing of the rub-ber is so extreme we could not bear it even driving through – and we do not live there day and night.

When we returned to the United States, Cynthia was still haunted by the conditions at the Firestone plantations. Living in Santa Barbara she was aware that Brooks Firestone is County Supervisor. She thought there was a unique opportunity for Firestone to change the worker's con-ditions, restore the land, make amends, and set new and visionary stan-dards for international corporations. Consequently, she and Bill Saa wrote a letter to Firestone in April 2006 and then arranged to meet with the Supervisor.

"In early May of 2006, my Liberian colleague and 'twin brother,' William Saa, and I had an unexpected opportunity to meet with Santa Barbara County Supervisor Brooks Firestone. When we arrived at his office, he invited us to sit down. We carefully sat on either side of the conference table, near the door, leaving the seat between us, at the head of the table, for him, but when he entered the room, he strode past us and sat at the head of the other end of the table, as far from us as possible. Outwardly polite and cordial, Supervisor Firestone quickly informed us he had not worked for the company since the 1970's, and that the family had sold both the company, and their name, to the Japanese tire maker, Bridgestone, in 1986. He told us that his grandfather, a good Christian, had only wanted the best for Liberia, and had, in addition to the rubber plantation and latex processing plant, built schools, roads and hospitals, only to lose everything. He told us that the Liberian people must now suffer for a time in order to show the world that they have progressed beyond violence. In his opinion, Liberia should be the first of the world's many beleaguered nations to seek a world power to re-colonize them, preferably China, India or the UK (with its impeccable record as a colonial power) and voluntarily relinquish their natural resources and their sovereignty in exchange for 'security' and a large occupying army. He flatly refused to meet with us again in the future. Although the letter that follows was never sent, it nonetheless articulates our vision for embracing the devastation of the past as a foundation for building a healthy future. It is our hope that this kind of conversation may yet be possible with Mr. Firestone, and others like him, one day soon."

April 12, 2006

Dear Mr. and Mrs. Firestone:

Greetings!

I am Cynthia Travis, Founder and President of the local Santa Barbara non-profit, **everyday gandhis**.[®] The purpose of the organization is to tell the story of how Peace is created. Our current focus is on Liberia, where we have been privileged to support and document traditional grassroots peacebuilding initiatives during that country's recent thrilling transition from hopeless civil war to a truly democratic peace. We produce a variety of written, internet, video, and still images; we support ongoing traditional peacebuilding councils and ceremonies; and we convene strategic 'wisdom councils', gatherings of diverse peacebuilders from the United States and around the world. It has been my great good fortune to work closely with Mr. William Saa, a renowned Liberian peacebuilder and trauma healing specialist.

I am writing today about a matter of the utmost urgency, with a proposal that I believe holds great possibility, a true 'win-win' scenario for all concerned. I hope you will agree and, if so, Mr. Saa and I look forward to meeting with you at your earliest convenience, as we believe this work to be time-sensitive as well as potentially far-reaching.

Based on your involvement in local humanitarian organizations, and your success in both the private sector and in public service, I know that you are generous and care about your community and the world. Your level of success speaks to a capacity to dream big dreams, and that is where I would like this conversation to take us. I will be frank and I hope you will bear with me:

When we are in Liberia (2-3 times a year), we work in Monrovia and in the town of Voinjama, near the Guinea border. In order to get to Voinjama, we drive past the Firestone Plantation. It is a huge operation, truly impressive, occupying nearly 10% of all arable land in Liberia. Unfortunately, it is also a terrible blight, and conditions are worse than deplorable. We have choked on the thick fumes that issue from the processing plant, and have seen the damage to the nearby Farmington River, upon which a great many people downstream depend for drinking water, irrigation and fishing. We have done extensive research and learned of the unbearable situation of the majority of people who live at the plantation, as well as the extensive pollution that flows downstream and eventually pours into a vast and sensitive wetlands that empties into prime sea turtle nesting ground where it meets the sea.

I understand the historical chain of events that led to the very advantageous lease to Harbel Firestone in the early 1900's. And I am aware that the plantation provided a refuge and steady income for those employed there during the war — although these advantages are not on a par with the damage done nor with the benefits to the Firestone company and, presumably, the family. I realize that the company has been sold to Bridgestone and that perhaps you may not have much, if any, direct involvement with the Liberian operation.

Nonetheless, if you could see what is there, you would be stunned and horrified. I know that these conditions are not of your direct making and that they do not reflect your core values. Still, the Firestone Plantation has come to represent all that is painful, illegal, and pitiless about Liberia's past. It is a lightning rod for bitterness, blame, and rising anti-American sentiment in a country that historically considers itself America's 'little brother' and greatest admirer.

We have become aware of the intense pressure, through lawsuits, negative publicity and the recent nonviolent labor strike, to redress these many regrettable, perhaps unintentional, but very real ills. It is our opinion, and that of all our most respected and knowledgeable colleagues, that Firestone cannot — and should not — avoid responsibility for rectifying everything that has gone wrong at the plantation.

A bleak picture, yes, and, ironically, this is exactly where the potential magic comes in:

Liberia is in a tremendously positive and, actually, astounding transition. This is a unique moment in that country's history, one that will likely set the future course not only for Liberia, but for the entire fragile sub-region.

Ellen Johnson Sirleaf, the newly elected President, has a sophisticated understanding of the complexities her government faces, and she has had the foresight to tap some of her country's greatest and most dedicated talent. Several trusted, highly skilled and breathtakingly dedicated colleagues (and some relatives of Mr. Saa's) are now serving in the new government. They are people of the highest integrity.

We believe that you have a once-in-a-lifetime opportunity to take the kind of action that could not only right the wrongs of the past, but could compound the Liberian miracle in unimaginable, perhaps incalculable, ways.

If, rather than resisting efforts to bring Firestone up to modern standards of decency, rather than letting the lawsuits take their course and the negative publicity build, you instead took sweeping, positive action now, we feel certain that you could accomplish the following:

Limit legal and financial liability; Avert a potential public relations disaster; Alleviate unnecessary suffering; Restore a vulnerable, precious and globally unique natural environment; Help over 20,000 people 'bootstrap' themselves to a better life literally overnight; Help insure the success of Liberia's newly elected democracy, thereby contributing directly to the future stability of all of West Africa; Restore a glow to the tarnished Firestone name and become, overnight, national, and possibly international heroes; Set the tone for a new trend of corporate responsibility that will make a real difference in people's lives, world peace and the future of the global environment.

Mr. Saa was in Liberia last month. His dear colleague, Kofi Woods, is the newly appointed Minister of Labor. (In early March, Mr. Woods successfully convinced more than 14,000 striking workers at Firestone to return to work because they trust that he is making every effort on their behalf.) We believe that by working directly with Mr. Woods and Liberia's highly informed and skillful environmental community, you could come to a discreet agreement that would free you/Bridgestone, the new government, the Firestone workers and their families, and the surrounding natural environment, from the painful legacy of the past. You are in a unique and extraordinary position, one that comes to few, if any, of us in our lifetimes. You could usher in a truly new time that would stand as a model for the world.

Mr. Woods is willing to come to California in the very near future. We would like to invite you to meet with us during that time. Please let us know when is the most convenient time to meet. This is such a special opportunity, and such a historic time.

We look forward so very much to speaking with you soon and to meeting in person. Please do not hesitate to call or write with any questions you may have.

Thank you in advance for what we hope and pray will be a joyful, extraordinary venture.

Sincerely,

Cynthia Travis and William F. Saa

everyday gandhis ®

Liberia with its coastline and what is left of the three-canopy rain forest was once a unique wildlife haven, the home to sea turtles, elephants, chimpanzees, etc. These natural resources have degenerated almost entirely due to war, pollution and hunting.

Much attention is being given to preventing war from breaking out again in this volatile area of West Africa where different armies of mercenaries, many of them child soldiers, allegedly ex-combatants, though they may not have given up their guns, gather, now on this border, now on that, waiting, for they are without education, livelihood or family. A new peace-building program that engages traditional healers and elders in an early warning system is being instituted by, among others, Tornorlah Varpilah who was with us in Chobe, Botswana. Elders, dreamers and medicine people are being asked to confer among themselves when they intuit danger and report what they fear to responsible authorities, including the United Nations peacekeeping forces. However, because of the environmental devastation, the medicines the traditional people need and the early warning signs they have used strategically for centuries are no longer available. The appearance of an elephant in a village was once a sign of peace coming. But almost all the elephants have been slaughtered for food and so they do not appear. Does this mean that we can't predict that peace is coming or that peace isn't possible until the elephant population is restored and protected? In Liberia we learned that peace building and healing were dependent upon restoring the environment and the indigenous values that are decimated by modern life.

എ

If 9/11 was our Reichstag fire as some say, then Katrina is our Chernobyl. Just as a few people are trying to return to New Orleans and other parts devastated by the hurricanes, despite the inability to clean up the toxic contamination, farming is being resumed in the Chernobyl area, because Ukrainian officials say the people have to return to their lives. Ukrainian scientists are claiming that the food grown there for the market is testing safe, they claim the beef from the cows is safe even though the milk is contaminated. Greenpeace calls it a whitewash. The local people do not/can not check their kitchen garden produce or the mushrooms and berries they glean from the forest for radiation. If they brought their food to be checked, they would have nothing to eat. The dense foliage absorbs radiation; the forests are highly radioactive. This is in marked contrast to the statement by the Chairman of the Chernobyl Affairs Committee at the Council of Ministers of the Republic of Belarus, in March 2004. Belarus took 70 percent of the fallout from the exploded power plant. Dr. Valentina Smolinkova testified that she never saw cancer in children before Chernobyl. "Those who say there is no link with Chernobyl should open their eyes and look at the medical statistics. Now cancer is common," she says "and many children with heart defects and kidney damage." Chernobyl may have been an accident but it is a continuing catastrophe with global consequences that increase because of our continual denial of reality.

At the twentieth anniversary of Chernobyl there is still much concern about the effects of radiation especially as the sarcophagus that has surrounded the reactor is sagging and in danger of breaking apart, at the very least, releasing a huge burst of radioactive dust and potentially sparking another explosion. The UK Independent reports that more than one-third of Britain still has significant contamination from the 1986 Chernobyl nuclear disaster, In Cumbria in northern England, thyroid cancers in children rose to 12 times the previous level.

Another article by Andrew Osborn and Geoffrey Lean, published: 23 April 2006 from the *Independent* begins:

"Twenty years ago this week, an unparalleled nuclear disaster struck. Its effects are still felt across Europe. As the West seeks to revive the technology, the anniversary sends a chill warning.

"She is known as 'Maria of Chernobyl' and — though she is not a saint — many view her birth in the shadow of the infamous reactor as little short of miraculous. Now aged six, Maria Vedernikova is the first and only child to be born in Chernobyl's post-catastrophe dead zone, a bleak and frightening area 18 miles in radius, now in Ukraine. Indeed, if you ask a guide at Chernobyl whether anyone has been born in the zone since 20 years ago this Wednesday, when the reactor exploded, you will get an emphatic '*nyet*'. The soil is poisoned with caesium and strontium. Only temporary workers and catastrophe tourists are allowed to enter for short periods at their own risk. ... And 'the zone' is associated in most people's minds with only one thing: death."

While the *New York Times* reported on April 20, 2006:

In Throats of Émigrés, Doctors Find a Legacy of Chernobyl

By RICHARD PÉREZ-PEÑA

The disaster struck 20 years ago on the other side of the world, in a nation that no longer exists, and the memory has faded in American minds. But the legacy of Chernobyl is turning up in hospitals and clinics in New York, where it is growing.

Cancer of the thyroid gland is rising in the United States, to about 30,000 new cases a year, according to the American Cancer Society and the National Cancer Institute, and it is climbing more sharply in New York State. While there are no data on the rates among different ethnic groups, doctors who work with émigrés from the former Soviet Union say that that population accounts for a significant part of the rise, because of the accident at the Chernobyl nuclear reactor in Pripyat, Ukraine, on April 26, 1986.

It has taken a long time to comprehend and acknowledge the extent and implications of Chernobyl and the same it seems will be true of the consequences of Katrina. In order for the consequences to be known, truths must be spoken. But government doesn't like to speak these truths, not at the moment, and not afterwards. We do not know the extent of the damage in New Orleans and we will never know. If we knew, we would probably hesitate before rebuilding as if no extreme measures need to be taken, and because we might have to acknowledge that we might be incapable of healing the situation now or in the future. This is certainly what happened in Russia but no one wanted to acknowledge it. What follows is from Joanna Macy's stunning book, *Widening Circles*.

"On the train, as we headed east from Minsk toward the Russian border, he [Harasch, a Russian psychologist] pulled out the map and told us the story once more. The burning reactor was a volcano of radioactivity when the winds shifted to the northeast, carrying the clouds of poisoned smoke in the direction of Moscow. To save the millions in the metropolitan area, a fast decision was taken to seed the clouds and cause them to precipitate. An unusually heavy late April rain, bearing intense concentrations of radioactive iodine, strontium, cesium and particles of plutonium drenched the towns and fields and forests of the Bryansk region, just across the Russian border from Chernobyl. The highest Geiger counter readings were measured as they still are, in and around the city of Novozybkov. 'The People there are not informed of their government's choice' …said Harasch." [xxvi]

It took four years for the Ukrainian commission experts to acknowledge that "the accident of the Chernobyl nuclear plant was, for its long-term consequences, the largest catastrophe of the contemporary era." Physicists Bella and Robert Belbéoch stated, "our views and hopes for a utopian and radiant future have vanished." They noted that scientific experts can no longer promise anything other than the management of catastrophes.

Katrina followed the tsunami in Asia but preceded Rita, Wilma, Alpha and Beta and the earthquake in Pakistan and India. The week before the medical conference, Wilma was heading toward Florida after battering the Yucatan for 24 hours making it the equivalent of three or four hurricanes, while Alpha was drenching the Dominican Republic. Towards the end of an official hurricane report predicting that Alpha would be absorbed into Wilma and both would batter the northeast coast of the U.S. and Canada, the weather reporter could not refrain from expressing shock. He or she wrote: "You can't make this stuff up." And then continued in official language: "Several tropical 'waves' are also under observation..."

When Katrina hit, many of us were already gravely alarmed about global warming, the tipping points that were becoming obvious. I did not quite realize that we had already entered the age of catastrophes, an ongoing series of interrelated tragic events that have consequences for each of us no matter where the location. To understand this is to understand that we have entered another reality. If we don't understand these events as systemic – if we do not see the ecology of disaster – we will miss what every physician and healer needs to know – the actual illness that he or she is truly called to heal.

"The looming privatization of the electrical power industry in Mexico jeopardizes all the rivers of Chiapas.

"In 1998 southern Mexico and Guatemala suffered extensive flooding and forest fires, damaging forest around Miramar and elsewhere in the selva and wreaking havoc along the lower Jatate. Hurricane rains in 1999 raised waters to record levels in the Usumacinta and Grijalva drainages, flooding the towns and villages of the Chontalpa, displacing thousands, and sending crocodiles, reportedly, into the streets."

— from Christopher Shaw [xxvii]

ও

In Liberia the devastation of war is obvious and ever-present. Health and peace are dependent upon restoring and protecting the environment. Holistic consciousness is required. So many people and beings on the globe are, this very moment, at war, are being terrorized, tortured, are hungry, homeless, in exile, in refugee camps, destitute, suffering, unhinged. This is the world we have been given to heal. We were once given little diseases, small and manageable plagues. Now the world's populations and all the beings are our patients. A challenge and the strange opportunity opens before us when we bear witness together in an alliance of hope and a willingness to see and act differently, to step away from the mind that creates catastrophes and step toward the kind of mind that is in affiliation by its nature with that which is whole.

ಀ

What follows is the poem I read at the American Academy for Environmental Medicine. The subject of the poem owns an organic farm next to the breeding places of the white pelicans and downwind of the pesticide sprays that undoubtedly did in the pelicans and the man as well. The poem does not state it explicitly, but after being tested negatively for a recurrence of cancer, it was discovered that this friend-farmer-environmentalist is suffering from a disintegrating bone condition that is the same as that which pelicans suffer from exposure to pesticides. His wife, also an environmentalist, noticed that the beautiful purple flower in the large photograph in the oncologist's waiting room is purple loose strife, an introduced plant, with a tenacious root system that chokes out other species, creating biologically unproductive monocultures that attract bees and butterflies to their blossoms, but offer no sustenance to higher life-forms.

PELICANS IN THE MIDWEST
(A Prose Poem)

The chicks died. Eight thousands of them. And you almost died too. And then it was revealed that you may be breaking the way so many fragile eggs broke, vulnerable as the bird nation to the poisons that erode the essential structures of our lives.

It is not enough to grieve, but to know the grief, its cause, its devastation, its imponderable effects upon everything it touches. We make a poison and cannot control its spread. It is a power with a mind of its own, it wants to be itself, and everything it touches dies, quickly in some cases, or over long, long stretches of time, a human lifetime, or longer, we do not know. And those, like yourself, who never made the poison, who stand against it, who cast a sacred circle to protect what is inside, who become the trees against an ill wind, still succumb. We can't protect the circle and the wind wasn't asked where to carry the powder. It wasn't asked where to set it down, or how to free itself from what it would never take up on its own.

What is the choice? To take the grief into ourselves, or to take the poison into ourselves, or both, on this terrible path we are asked to carve toward a different kind of knowledge than the kind we have been taught to gather to us and to call power. Knowledge is power, we were told.

This is not power. Look how the white powder has made a powder of our bones. Look how the egg dissolves at the slightest tremor. Look how it cannot protect or sustain what it loves.

I try to write this and I have only music to offer. A certain music in the rhythm or the arrangement of words alongside each other so that they become companions to a vision too far away to see. We do not know *and* it depends entirely on us. And then the song I never knew before takes me and I hear the words I wouldn't know to speak:

The challenge is to become the pelican though we have never entered the territory of Pelican mind. Grief is the shimmering cry that can bind us to each other so exactly that there will be no distinction between one thought, one being, and another, the way the pelicans glide together upon the lower breezes and currents in graceful lines that simultaneously display their acquiescence and their intent.

Like the pelican, we look down at our chicks and watch them die. We observe helplessly – that is our calling. If we pretend for a moment that there is something we can do, we will have lost contact with Pelican mind. Making this connection, difficult as it may seem, is what we can do. So then let us observe hopelessly as they must do. You – I – we must do this. We must be helpless for a long time and then, afterwards, when we pick up our lives, we will not pick up anything at all that will do harm. We will not weigh one harm against another, or one creature or one species. We will not choose the immediate over the long run or this moment over the future. We will not choose the lesser of two evils; we will not be expedient or resigned. We will not.

Such a garment of sorrow you are asked to wear. Such a delicate silk woven from your own body, your own tears, from a storm of feathers. A strange raiment that will never be a fashion. Yet, clad this way, you will do everything for these little ones, our beloveds, your chicks, your babes, now flesh of your flesh. Yes your babes, their little lives, your little ones, your own body, your little life, all our little lives.

❧

I have been looking for the antonym for catastrophe, which means the end of a story. There is no exact opposite but there are the words – prelude and overture. We know what the preludes to catastrophe have been. What might prelude the end of war? What might prelude healing? What might be the preludes to the restoration of the natural world?

These are the questions we have been given to carry.

We cannot carry these questions alone. We have to carry them together. When wise people are confronted by situations that are beyond them, they admit their incapacity and they call councils. We must call councils. We must call the elders, wise ones, scientists, et al., the experienced ones of the world community to confer with us and each other.

Daré and **everyday gandhis** are beginning to call councils. We are preparing to host councils of peace builders and visionaries. This, in anticipation, also, of councils of environmentalists.

A Dream, January 2006:

> *Two men have come to study with me and then there is a third. The two are from Africa and when I wonder what we might offer them, I learn that one is the son of a chief and both have been educated in the old ways and so I agree to work with them. As I do not want to discuss anything, even their participation, outside of the circle, I ask the circle to be called and everyone gathered. As we are waiting, the third man, an Israeli, begins speaking about something that is angering him. One of the African men answers him and they enter into a conflicted discourse so endemic to the public discourse. I have to ask them to stop because they are out of council and we cannot continue this way. In this manner that they are speaking, I say, there is argument and the desire to convince someone of something that is not the way of the circle. The way of the council circle is not*

arguing or being right or wrong, but coming to understanding. People are slow to gather because some are involved in a musical ritual of healing. But there has been contention and we need to call the spirits and sit in council. I understand that sitting in council is even more urgent than finishing the healing ritual though it involves so many of the essential people.

It is not only that the issues we face require that we address them in council; it is that in council we see our ongoing and essential interdependence.

და

Because we don't know what to do, we turned to the animals and asked them to sit in council with us. Then the elephants came.

I will try to speak of it here even though there can be no words for this advent.

და

The Coming of the Ambassadors, September 2005

The first day, September 16, 2005, we went out by boat. We passed two of the corpses of elephants in the river. The causes of the sudden deaths of elephants, babies and adults are unknown but environmental devastation (so many elephants in so small a corridor), along with anthrax from the grazing cattle introduced into the area, is suspected.

(The next week as we were taxied from the airport to a small hotel in Monrovia, Liberia, we would pass the body of an old man in the street alongside a small stream where children were playing and men were fishing. Civil war and environmental deterioration have made death commonplace. Neither the park guide accompanying us nor the taxi driver volunteered any commentary on the dead.)

There was a bull elephant standing on a tiny island in the river. A white egret was poised at his feet. We stayed with him a long time. He was still, the bird was still, and we were stilled. We thought this might be a first sighting.

The second day, now without a guide and in our rented 4x4s, we went to the place where we had first sighted the Ambassador at 5 p.m. on Epiphany, January 6th 2000. We stopped, as we had then, at what we since have called the Chapungu tree. Because the white peace eagle, the Chapungu, had landed there, we stopped there again. We had watched then as the elephant approached us with solemn deliberation and engaged us in an undeniable ritual of acknowledgement.

This time the bull elephant was waiting for us at the tree. We stopped and greeted him the way we had before. We stayed in medi-

Chapungu, the peace eagle.
Photo by Cyndie Travis, Chobe 9/2006

tation together for a long time. Suddenly, he trumpeted loudly and the camera people scampered quickly back into the closed cab of the truck as I remained with a few others in the open back. An answering trumpet startled us further. I could sense the fear of some of those with me in the open. It was essential not to be afraid. No matter what happens, I thought, do not be afraid. This is a time when we have to enact trust. Then a small herd of cows and calves came down directly alongside our trucks to the river; this we understood as a gesture of trust on the part of the elephants. We also agreed that if we didn't see the Ambassador again, we would be entirely satisfied and confirmed with this visit.

Each day, we went to the Chapungu tree at 5 p.m. In the days that followed, we met two bull elephants walking together, clearly friends and companions. Valerie had dreamed them and, as only the two of us were there together, we recognized that two partners were greeting two partners in the work of bringing healing to the world, an alliance being forged among the four of us. One day, the bull elephant came out from the river bank and walked toward me so deliberately, looking me directly in the eye that Valerie said she could feel the love he felt for me, but perhaps what she felt was the awe and gratitude and love that I was feeling in his presence. Another day, the bull elephant was courting a female and we watched them as their trunks intertwined and he caressed her back. It was time for us to leave which we did gladly, not wishing to interfere in their mating ritual.

One morning, we came upon a long single file of fifty elephants or more, the matriarch in the lead and the littlest elephant, only several months old, behind. They looked exactly like the line on the billboard outside the Preserve that said, "Follow our lead."

Photo by Cynthia Travis

Joking with Paul Lynch, the videographer, I asked him to roll back the clock and get the sequence when we returned to the park in the afternoon. And as it happened, when we entered the park we did see the matriarch leaving the water hole and the elephants organizing themselves in such a file again that I had never seen before or since.

On the last day, we went toward the Chapungu tree when Michael noticed a white eagle flying toward another tree and we followed it, stopping where it landed not too far away. It was 5 p.m. and this was our last hour in the park. The bull elephant, the Ambassador, was at the river's edge, seemingly oblivious to us. The four of us who were there then, Valerie, Michael, Cyndie and myself, meditated and prayed. Then a female with three calves of different ages came down to him at the river. The young ones frolicked while she and he turned toward each other and rubbed their trunks in gestures of greeting and affection. Then the female, without grazing or drinking, turned to leave but the littlest elephant, a bull, wanted to stay. In a most unusual gesture of parental affection and sweet discipline, the older bull approached the little one and gently nudged his buttocks until he followed after his mother.

I began to understand something inexplicable. All the time that I was in Botswana, and for years earlier, I had been praying for alliance with the animals and other beings of the natural world because I am horrified that human beings are devastating the natural world. However, these ambassadors responded by showing us the sweetness and intelligence of their communal lives. So we become the ambassadors to a great people; I think of them now as Speakers for the Wild.

The bull turned from us and walked the short distance to the Chapungu tree. We followed and stopped at a safe and unobtrusive distance. He was seemingly preoccupied with the grasses alongside him but he didn't take any to eat. Then we saw that he was swinging his trunk over a large object, a stone probably, but what we could not quite discern. And then he picked it up and threw it toward us in an unmistakable gesture of offering us a gift. He moved further along the river, deliberately stepped into a small declivity, went down on his knees as one does in prayer, then rose up, twisted his trunk into the impossible knot that Michael and I had first seen in 2000 when he came toward us. Then he trumpeted one last time and disappeared into the brush. It was exactly 6 p.m., the time we had to leave the preserve. I ran out of the car to pick up the gift…an old and weathered thighbone of an elephant.

As Barbara Gowdy had written in her novel about elephants *The White Bone*:

"None of the humans who passed the boulders ever spotted it, even though, over the years, it bleached to a blinding whiteness. Meanwhile it radiated toward all living creatures a quality of forgiveness and hope. But the hearts of humans were hard, and would not be pierced. Not then."[xxviii]

And as I wrote at the end of my letter to her:

"It was not a rib bone. It is a femur. It is not blinding white. Still it was thrown to us by a he-one."

Photo by Cynthia Travis

ო

MANDLOVU MIND

Suddenly, I am of a single mind extended
Across an unknown geography,
And imprinted, as if by a river, on the moment.
A mind held in unison by a large gray tribe
Meandering in reverent concert
Among trees, feasting on leaves.
One great eye reflecting blue
From the turn inward
Toward the hidden sky that, again,
Like an underground stream
Continuously nourishes

What will appear after the dawn
Bleaches away the mystery in which we rock
Through the endless green dark.

I am drawn forward by the lattice,
By a concordance of light and intelligence
Constituted from the unceasing and consonant
Hum of cows and the inaudible bellow of bulls,
A web thrumming and gliding
Along the pathways we remember
Miles later or ages past.

I am, we are,
Who can distinguish us?
A gathering of souls, hulking and muddied,
Large enough – if there is a purpose –
To carry the accumulated joy of centuries
Walking thus within each other's
Particular knowing and delight.

This is our grace: To be a note
In the exact chord that animates creation,
The dissolve of all the rivers
That are both place and moment,
An ocean of mind moving
Forward and back,
Outside of any motion
Contained within it.

This is particle and wave. How simple.
The merest conversation between us

Becoming the essential drone
Into which we gladly disappear.
A common music, a singular heavy tread,
Ceaselessly carving a path,
For the waters tumbling invisibly
Beneath.
I have always wanted to be with them,
With you,
So.

Gratitude and Blessings.

Topanga
April 22, 2006
Earth Day

This poem by Deena is on Jami Sieber's "Hidden Sky" album. Jami Sieber went to Thailand to play cello with the Thailand Elephant Orchestra. Some of these original compositions include the elephant musicians. See Out Front Music: http://www.jamisieber.com/

Mandlovu is the word the Ndebele people of Zimbabwe use for female elephant. It is connected in resonance with the Mambo Kadze, the name for the deity that is both elephant, the Virgin Mary and the Great Mother.

AFTERWORD

LET US MAKE A PILGRIMAGE TO THE FUTURE

$\mathcal{F}$our of us, Cynthia Travis, Nancy Myers, Carolyn Raffensperger and I, met with Krystyna Jurzykowski at her home, High Hope, adjacent to Fossil Rim Wildlife Center, a preserve and research center for endangered African animals in Glen Rose, Texas. One of our purposes, as was suggested in "Katrina – Our Chernobyl" was to explore the possibilities of calling environmentalists into council on behalf of the current environmental crisis. Cynthia and I had thought that being on the land, telling dreams, engaging in ritual, calling on the spirits and ancestors, experiencing sanctuary while accessing the collective wisdom might bring new vision to those who are on the front lines of the dread news that is revealed each day.

Twice during our visit we went to Fossil Rim to visit with the animals, especially the rhinoceroses, who, Krystyna told us, have a lineage of 65 million years.

The second day, a black rhinoceros slipped into her mud wallow as we approached, rolled around until she was on her back with her short legs waving in the air in what surely was pure joy. When I got out of the car, she was upright again and approached me directly as I neared her pen. How to imagine anything but that we were confirming an appointment?

Soon, she put her head through the steel ropes that formed the pen as I reached out to stroke her behind the ears where the tender places are. Her horn was covered with mud and I removed some of it and rubbed it on the skin where she could not reach. I held her by the cheeks as if she were a small child and sometimes she rested her lower lip on the cables so that I could press grass into her mouth. The heritage of two tons, four thousand pounds, 65 million years in my hands! I cannot translate into words what transpired between us. It may take years to really understand; I prefer to wait until it reveals itself. I do not want to impose my thinking upon our intimate connection.

Then we both knew instantly our meeting was over. We disengaged easily and she, inexplicably, began moving backwards while continuing

Photo by Krystyna Jurzykowski

to make eye contact though I have been assured rhinos don't see well. I moved backwards as well, learning as best as I could the etiquette that honored the moment. And then she stopped and bowed her head but not to graze. She formally bowed her head. I went down on my hands and knees and bowed my head to the ground. We both raised our heads at the same time. She turned away. I turned away. It was over. In a few minutes, she approached Nancy who had her own sweet encounter with her.

A few feet away, Cyndie was singing to another rhinoceros, a male who was, it seemed, enchanted.

I walked into the field to say my prayers of gratitude. The teachings repeat themselves: Learn from the animals and the beings of the natural world. Make alliances.

℅

Some days later, Carolyn Raffensperger had a remarkable dream that helps to confirm our belief that we will have a future and that future beings, like ancestors, are among us, and sustain us in the daily work of restoration. Carolyn writes:

"Over the last 25 years I've been seeking new ideas and actions that would lay a path for true environmental protection. The old way of measuring and managing risk has led to global warming, emptying the oceans, polluting every corner of the world with toxic chemicals and increasing chronic diseases in humans.

"A central idea that emerged in the last decade is the precautionary principle: the simple notion that a stitch in time saves nine. In other words, we can take precautionary action to prevent harm in the face of uncertainty.

"My indigenous friends have long said that the precautionary principle is the Seventh Generation Principle, which comes from the Six Nations Iroquois Confederacy practice of making decisions with the seventh generation in mind. The only way we can guarantee that we leave blessings and an inheritance for future generations rather than visiting upon them our sins is to use the precautionary principle and make decisions that are the wisest, fairest, most preventive of harm.

"Last October, my friend Bob Shimek called and asked how we could apply these ideas to mining on tribal lands. It occurred to me that we could do more than make decisions considering future generations; we could actually locate that responsibility in specific people. We can designate guardians for future generations through elections, appointments and anointings."§

℀

Guardians for the future. Do you see that we are in a council? A council that began many years ago, whether we have met each other or not, and that continues, even here, on these pages. What makes it a true council is that it includes the future beings.

Guardianship is not a new idea. It is an idea that is flowering now. Joanna Macy began thinking of her Guardianship project in the 70s and then later in the 80s:

> [The roots of *The Nuclear Guardianship Project for the Responsible Care of Radioactive Wastes*] started with a kind of vision I had in England in 1983, when I visited the peace camps that had spontaneously arisen around nuclear bases - Greenham Common, Molesworth, Porton Down, Upper Heyford, and many others. I went on a pilgrimage to four of these places after a month's lecture and workshop tour, and when I was there I sensed that I was on sacred ground. I had a feeling of déjà vu. I thought, "Oh, maybe I'm being reminded of the

---

§ *See the Appendix, The Bemidji Statement on Seventh Generation Guardianship.*

monasteries that kept the flame of learning alive in the Middle Ages." People made pilgrimages to those places too.

Greenham Common. The name gives us pause. When we were together at Fossil Rim, Nancy Myers also had a vision of being with women on behalf of the earth in the manner of the women of Greenham Commons. Afterwards we called her "Commoner." She and Carolyn Raffensperger have been working on applications of the law of the Commons for our time.

But then I [Joanna] realized, "No, this is about the *future*. This is how the radioactive remains are going to be guarded for the sake of future beings, through the generations, through the centuries, through the millennia – because the radioactivity must be kept out of the biosphere. And it can only be kept out by the attention of the *human mind*, watching. They're going to *guard* it, and the guardian sites will be places of remembering and mindfulness, places to which people make pilgrimage." The logic of it became very clear to me then. [xxix]

Guardians Of The Future: The Nuclear Guardianship Project is a grassroots program for handling nuclear waste — and deepening our relationship to time. An Interview with Joanna Macy, by Alan Atkisson:

"Being concerned for the people and creatures who will come after us means opening to the experience of what Macy calls 'deep time' — taking in the reality of the time spans during which nuclear wastes will continue to be a hazard. Here she explains deep time, the Guardianship Project, and why humans have to stick around for the next couple of hundred millennia.

'[After the first war in the Persian Gulf] at first I felt a sense of futility. I felt paralyzed, almost, for days — like a rabbit or deer frozen in the headlights of a car.

'It took some time, and some grieving, and some deep breathing. I realized then that the war in no way changed the picture — except that it changed the context in which we were mounting these other efforts, by dramatizing more clearly the importance of the work that we undertake on behalf of life. More than ever, we are called to be guardians in every sense of the word.

'We're called to be guardians of truth, for one thing. When we

see how facts are manipulated and misrepresented — as we are, in fact, deluged with lies — the extraordinary gift of consciousness, the attentive mind and the mindful heart, become perhaps the most precious of gifts. So whether we're talking about truth, or something like the seeds that we need to maintain a varied agriculture, what more important task do we have but to guard these things for the sake of future beings — to carry them forward?'"
http://www.context.org/ICLIB/IC28/Macy.htm

Joanna's work continues with The Great Turning, "a name for the essential adventure of our time: the shift from the Industrial Growth Society to a life-sustaining civilization."

"A revolution is underway because people are realizing that our needs can be met without destroying our world. We have the technical knowledge, the communication tools, and material resources to grow enough food, ensure clean air and water, and meet rational energy needs. Future generations, if there is a livable world for them, will look back at the epochal transition we are making to a life-sustaining society. And they may well call this the time of the Great Turning. It is happening now.

"... Whether or not it is recognized by corporate-controlled media, the Great Turning is a reality. Although we cannot know yet if it will take hold in time for humans and other complex life forms to survive, we can know that it is under way. And it is gaining momentum, through the actions of countless individuals and groups around the world. To see this as the larger context of our lives clears our vision and summons our courage."
http://www.joannamacy.net/html/great.html

☙

Carolyn's letter responding to her dream continues: "I went to visit Krystyna at Fossil Rim with Cynthia, Nancy and Deena. In my conversation with the rhinos they told me that since they've been around for 65 million years they could imagine thousands of generations to come. I asked if we could start with seven and work up from there.

"When I returned from Fossil Rim and was in the midst of the usual work flurry and difficulties I had the following dream:

I am in another world and another time, seated at a table with a woman across from me, she like a fortune-teller, and I, the supplicant. We have spilled gorgeous golden, raspberry-pink sand-like material on the table. She is scraping up every bit and putting it into open shells. I want to make sure we get it all and not waste any of the beauty. She shimmers with a gold light. We are time travelers: the pink sand is sprinkled on us and we move through time. We time travelers recognize each other by the golden light. We have gone back into the past to help change things so the future will be [is] better – more whole, more beautiful. We were charged by future generations to set the compass direction for this generation so there would be a future.

Nearby a nondescript older, red-haired man is resting in a casual crouch on the ground. He says, "We have a bond. What is between us? Were we married in a previous life?" I am just about to make a casual, dismissive remark and go on since he does not interest me. But I realize that I need to stop and fully look at him. If I get still, I will know what our relationship is. I gather myself and attend to his being. No we weren't married in a previous life, we were married in a future life.

Around us, many other golden women were moving through the sun-charged light.

"The future will be taken care of. There will be a future. We have been charged."

ↄ

Let us make a pilgrimage to the future and the future beings. The future beings came to Joanna some years ago and now they have come to Carolyn. What happens if we each invite then to be with us, to guide us? Pilgrimage is a call to the heart. One never knows when there will be summons from Spirit. But in responding, we become the one who answers such a call as the response coheres a dialogue between the individual and the numinous or the Divine. And the call? How does one recognize it? That is also mysterious.

This book has been about pilgrimage. Pilgrimage as a way of bearing witness and pilgrimage as a way of acting on behalf of the future.

This book ended on Earth Day April 22nd 2006. But then it picked up again. History had claims on me and on it and I yielded to them.

I did not know that April 26ᵗʰ 2006 was the 20ᵗʰ anniversary of the explosion at the nuclear plant in Chernobyl. But suddenly, as I was writing and rewriting this piece, in the circular manner of association, I understood that I have been deeply involved in ways I had not recognized in the matter of the use of nuclear energy. The title, "Katrina – Our Chernobyl," had come to me and I had accepted it without thinking that I was being taken on a journey.

Katrina, as I have said before, took me down and when I spoke to the American Academy of Environmental Medicine, I had no choice but to reveal my broken heart about Katrina and about Chernobyl. I carried a focus and spoke with an urgency I didn't myself fully understand. Later, as I began this essay, such urgency returned. Some of it was internal as some of it was the consequence of the synchronicity of circumstances.

The approaching 20ᵗʰ anniversary was the occasion for scientists and writers who had been relatively silent to speak out about the utter devastation and unending danger that had resulted from the explosion. Additionally, the grotesque birth defects and other horrific consequences of depleted uranium usage in Afghanistan were just making themselves known while President Bush, quagmired in Iraq and in the quicksand and rubble of civilian and military deaths, lies, illegalities, crimes, tortures, unethical conduct, and unparalleled corruption, began threatening a nuclear strike against Iran's fledgling nuclear interests. The psychosis inherent in the military political situation revealed itself in the deep disconnect between the irreparable damage of nuclear weapons and energy and the U.S. government's insistence on using them – and its insistence on using them to prevent them from being used.

When I read that members of the Western Shoshone Nation were organizing to protest and refuse a planned Defense Department explosion of a 700 ton bunker buster bomb that threatens to raise a mushroom cloud of buried radioactive dust in an explosion that could have the same effects as Chernobyl, I felt called to the Nevada atomic test site, where a cousin by marriage had, as a member of the army, been blasted by radiation from a test, and had died relatively soon afterwards of leukemia.

There was no time for me to refuse the call or to engage in elaborate preparations. Of nine who wanted to go, four of us were able, including Danelia Wild, Elenna Rubin Goodman, (who, with her husband

Garner MacAleer, as mentioned earlier in this book, carries the Oakland Daré) and Ayelet Berman Cohen. We had only the weekend of May 6th and 7th. We picked up Elenna at the Las Vegas airport. We had air mattresses and sleeping bags, some snacks and water, a bare change of clothes, rattles and ritual items. We had no reservations, no connections, no plans. Of the five others who had wanted to join us and couldn't, four suddenly became too ill to go. One of those, Michael, my husband, asked a question that would guide us on the journey: What is the medicine each one of you is carrying to this work?

Ayelet, had, seven months earlier, when Ed Tick was among us, first recognized that, as an Israeli, she lived with constant war within her. Wracked by this knowledge, she had decided to forbid her sons to return to Israel as they would be required to serve in the army. In the last months, she had tracked ten years of dreams that had over time revealed the internal wars and the antidotes to them. She was coming with us as someone entirely committed to applying dream wisdom and learning the true ways of peacemaking.

Two weeks before, Ayelet had a dream in which I became an old, old woman acting on behalf of the earth.

I can barely recognize her. She does all kinds of miracles and magic. She is an old magician. I look at her and try to see the Deena that I know.

One of Deena's eyes is missing. (The Hebrew word soomah, meaning "blind in one eye" repeats itself in the dream). The right side of Deena's face, where the eye is missing, is beaten up, black and blue. The empty space in her eye socket looks like a crater.

"Materialism is over," declares the old, blind Deena as she walks between the people carrying a tiny stick in her hand. I am there. Deena breaks the word "materialism" into syllables. "Ma - ter - i - al - ism is over." I ask her: "Who are you?" And she says: "I am talking from another dimension. I ask her if she died and she says: "No. I speak from the point of view of the blind, of the "soomah." "We are all blind." Now, very dramatically like a witch in a play, while the crowd is closing in on her, she says: "Materialism has died in the world. We cannot afford to want more and more things. We are blind to the condition of the earth. I took out my eye as an act of solidarity with the earth that wants to teach us about our blindness." I ask silently - did you do this to yourself, and she answers to the crowd. "With a hot iron poker, a symbolic poker."

This is a performance, a part of a play that Deena wrote and di-

rected. *She is the main character in her own play. The old Deena continues: "The earth is wearing a mask too. No human can really hurt the essence of the earth. Mother Earth is beyond the reach of humans. The earth has put on a mask of suffering to teach us a lesson."*

I ask silently: What is the lesson? "Greed, hate, hate, jealousy, revenge, hate, revenge, everything that eats human beings from the inside. This is the time for purification."

There are three acts to Deena's play. The first act is the holy nature of the earth. The second is the greed of humanity. The third is the purification process. There is opportunity to change and be changed.

Deena takes off her mask and I see the Deena I know. Everyone applauds.

At the end of the dream/play, Rudolf Steiner* comes in and talks about peacemaking. He speaks about the need for purification before any peace process is possible. He offers the teaching: there is no peace without peace. Ein shalom blee shalom.

(*Ayelet Berman Cohen sends her children to a Waldorf School based on the principles of Rudolf Steiner. She is also helping to support a Waldorf School and Peace Center in Israel for Israeli Jews and Arabs.)

A few hours after I wrote this, the following came to me in an e-mail:

For This Michael Age
by Rudolf Steiner

We must eradicate from the soul
All fear and terror of what comes toward one
out of the future.
We must acquire serenity in all feelings and sensations
about the future.
We must look forward with absolute equanimity
to all that may come,
And we must think only,
that whatever comes is given to us
by a world direction full of wisdom.

It is part of what we must learn in this age, namely,
to live out of pure trust,
without any security in existence,
trust in the ever-present help of the spiritual world.
Truly, nothing else will do,

> if our courage is not to fail us.
>
> Let us discipline our will,
> And let us seek the awakening from within ourselves,
> Every morning
> And every evening.

The day before we left, Danelia, Carol and I had witnessed a long death agony of a harmless gopher snake cut in two by a panicked meter man. For almost an hour, the head writhed open mouthed in what was unmistakably a silent scream while the body twisted toward the head in useless attempts to reconnect itself. Danelia, who had over years of initiation committed herself to serving and carrying community while equally reverent before the too numerous road kills and other animal murders, had come to the deep understanding that the creatures and beings of the earth are as inherently members of the community as are the humans.

Finally, Elenna was coming to recognize that ritual alliance with the spirits is as tactical and pragmatic an activity as any humanly devised political action. For myself, I was acting on the prayer and hope that the past evidence of true and conscious alliances with the earth, the natural world, the living beings and elementals, might augur other possibilities under these circumstances.

Each of us, thus, was being called to soul searching and initiation even as we were trying to engage in political and healing activity.

This final story brings us to grief and vision at the threshold of the unknown. What is unknown is whether we can restore creation. However, if we can, it will only be with the allies, grief and vision. And so we went as mourners. And so we went willing, also, to carry and affirm the imagination of possibility.

There were unusual cloud formations in the sky and I chose to follow them. What if they were a holy script? We stopped at one site, wondering if we should put down our sleeping bags there, but the clouds had formed arrows and so we went on.

Markers at the highway and then up the dirt road that looked like prayer flags led us to an entirely private campsite overlooking the entirely empty, silent, probably ruined and radiant, lifeless desert valley, with a fire pit at its center, a mile and a half from the road. There we slept within a medicine wheel under the stars and moon. Elenna carrying fire, the heart, at the south; Ayelet carrying water, the dream, at the west; Danelia carrying stone and life force, the earth, at the north, while I carried vision, the air, at the east.

When we gathered in ritual in the morning, I was praying that all the beings and elementals might gather in council to create an energy and intelligence capable of refusing any great harm that might be enacted against the earth. I was praying that nothing of the earth could ever again be used to enact great harm against the earth, against the mother. At that moment, a wild wind rose abruptly and flung our mattresses, sleeping bags and all possessions into the air and hurled them sixty feet or more – and then it calmed.

Soon after, sanctifying a peace pipe, offering prayer smoke to the spirits and the directions, I was so dizzied by the first small puff, I reeled and staggered, as if I had been struck, until I dropped to my knees and found myself sobbing uncontrollably upon the radioactive earth, the mother condemned to the eternity of the unquenchable fire. My grief, our grief, and the sense of the elementals responding, confirmed my belief, our belief, that the impossible is possible, that creation can and will be restored – because – the animals, the elementals and the spirits are joining together with the humans whose hearts are broken in a common purpose. Of course, the entire process of creating alliances with other beings is a long one that may take hundreds of years. Do we have enough time? This question distracts us. As it may take a long time, we are being called to start now.

During the last moments of silence before we left the site, Elenna discovered that a more distant fire pit had empty bullet shells in it. Crushed and pocked aluminum cans had been punctured by buckshot. This had not been a peace camp as we had thought. The prayer flags were only plastic markers. We can look at it that way. Or we can assume that we had been invited into what could become a peace camp and our prayers and activities had helped to make it so.

As we gathered ourselves to return on Sunday afternoon, a monochromatic, sand colored, unmarked lizard, one of two we had seen, that with two ravens and a hidden single tiny bird cheeping in the brush, and the most minute and yet exquisite purple flower, the size and fragrance of a drop of water, were the only living beings we came across in this refuge. These few beings and a great white cloud in the shape of a bird, or a spirit or an angel that had been with us since dawn and stayed until we left.

Photo ©2006 Ayelet Berman Cohen

The lizard rushed into the roadway as if to cross it but positioned itself upon a stone as if offering a sermon and so we gathered around it for half an hour. Researching it later, the only lizard I could find that resembled it was identified by the *Audubon Society Field Guide to North American Reptile and Amphibians* as the Bleached Earless Lizard, "restricted to White Sands region, (Otero county)" New Mexico, the Trinity test site where the first nuclear bombs had been exploded.

We had come in prayer. Urgency had brought us, but we didn't know if our presence could protect or heal anything. Foolishness or faith? How often I ask myself this question.

We did not know exactly why we had come, what we were to do, or what the consequences of our journey might be. Soon, however, it was time to leave. We asked the I Ching to guide us one more time.

Who are we to become? How are we to proceed? What is possible?

Hexagram 26, Great Accumulates/Gathering the Spirit, describes your situation in terms of having a central idea that defines what is valuable.

Eliminate the negativity now. Renovate a corrupt situation. Commit yourself to what you truly believe in. Focus on a single idea and use that to impose a direction on your life.

In order for a ritual to matter, it must have our life behind it. We must offer ourselves entirely to its possibility.

When we returned home, we learned that fifteen Western Shoshone Spirit Runners had been circumambulating the 240 mile perimeter of the Nevada Nuclear Test Site.

"Through our prayers and with the help of other people, we will keep more nuclear waste from our lands," said Johnnie Bobb, the Western Shoshone National Council member, artist and spiritual leader.[xxx]

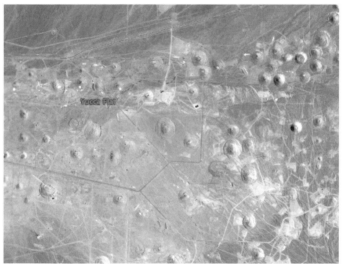

The Nevada Test Site, Courtesy Google Earth, 2006
Altitude, approx. 11 miles, 37°N 06′, 116°W 02

On May 11th the federal government announced it would delay the blast for at least three weeks to resolve a legal challenge.

Focus on a single idea. Use that to impose a direction on your life. Concentrate everything on this goal. Gather all the different parts of yourself and all your many encounters. Take the long view. Develop an atmosphere in which things can grow. This is the right time to enter the Stream of Life with a purpose and to embark on significant enterprises. [xxxi]

On May 26, 2006, the National Nuclear Security Administration announced that it was postponing the tests indefinitely.

TEST EXPLOSION IN NEVADA PUT ON INDEFINITE HOLD, by Robert Gehrke, *The Salt Lake Tribune*

WASHINGTON: Divine Strake, a massive explosives test originally planned for next month, has been put on indefinite hold.

The National Nuclear Security Administration said Friday it was postponing the test.... Questions about the test were raised by Nevada environmental officials, Sen. Orrin Hatch and Rep. Jim Matheson, and in a lawsuit that includes Utah Downwinders, who were sickened by fallout from Cold War nuclear testing.

"We have always been concerned about background radiation at the site. We have been repeatedly told, even during my staff's visit to the site, that this was not a concern," Sen. Orrin Hatch said in a statement. "But since we've asked them to back up their conclusions with scientific evidence, it looks like our concerns are justified." National Nuclear Security Administration said Friday that it would withdraw its original finding that the test would not have any significant environmental impact so it can provide additional information regarding "background levels of radiation." "After reading comments about 'mushroom clouds' and 'low yield nuclear weapons', I was greatly concerned, and expressed as much to the director of DTRA [Defense Threat Reduction Agency]," Matheson said in a statement. "I advised him to put all the health and safety data out on the table so that people's fears about being once again exposed to radioactive contamination could be addressed. I am very pleased to see that these agencies have acted on my advice." The agency said it will determine how to best proceed after it decides how to address the questions raised by interested parties.

Rep. Rob Bishop, R-Utah, said there was no harm in postponing the test. "We need to make sure the concerns that have been raised have been satisfied before moving on with that," he said.

Divine Strake was originally scheduled for June 2, but was postponed after the Pentagon and the National Nuclear Security Administration were sued by the Utah Downwinders and a Nevada Indian tribe.... The goal is to measure the ground tremors that would be produced by such a blast, and use the information to build computer models to simulate explosions.

Originally, Defense Department budget documents said that the test would help war planners choose the smallest possible nuclear weapon to destroy buried and fortified targets, but the Pentagon later said that the inclusion of the word "nuclear" in the document was a mistake.

The blast would use explosives similar to those used in the bombing of the Oklahoma City federal building, but the blast would be 280 times larger. It would also be nearly 50 times larger than the biggest known conventional weapon in the U.S. arsenal and on par with the smallest U.S. nuclear weapons.

That fact, along with efforts by the Bush administration to repeal a ban on development of low-yield nuclear weapons, prompted concern from nonproliferation advocates that the aim was to create new tactical nuclear weapons.

This is moving on the Great Way. The energy has accumulated. You are walking Heaven's highway. Your sacrifice is accepted and blessings will flow. There is no doubt about your success.

ᴄ⌇

We cannot know, of course, if our pilgrimage, or the running prayers of the Shoshone people, or the prayers of the "downwinders" had any effect on what transpired in government. Perhaps the postponement that we hope is forever is due entirely to the legal actions and political pressures. But we do not know. We know only that we were called and we answered and that the divinations were so particular and exact we felt as if we were being addressed directly.

When we were advised by Great Accumulates/Gathering the Spirit, we each meditated alone trying to understand who and what we were being asked to become and how we were to live our lives.

Focus on a single idea. Use that to impose a direction on your life. Concentrate everything on this goal.

And perhaps if we align ourselves with Spirit, creation will be restored.

This is moving on the Great Way. The energy has accumulated. You are walking Heaven's highway. Your sacrifice is accepted and blessings will flow. There is no doubt about your success.

༄

The Results of Council

When we speak of council, we emphasize several ideas:

Indigenous people worldwide have met in council when they have been troubled by circumstances that were greater than their capacity to meet them. Indigenous people have met in council when they were endangered and didn't know what to do.

The gifts one brings to council are the ability to listen and the prayer that someone who speaks will have some of the wisdom that the tribe requires and that the wisdom among the participants will come together to reveal something new and useful.

In Topanga, when we sit in council, we listen and then we speak to the question by sharing stories, events, anecdotes and experiences. The stories come together, they create a weaving, a tapestry and soon we find ourselves in a different field of understanding. Such is, I hope the experience of reading this book. It is what it is because of the different voices, the different beings, the ancestors and the future beings and because of the ways the themes weave in and around so that we see, as the native people of North America continually remind us, the connection between all beings, so that we live in terms of *all my relations*.

༄

When Maria Pollia brought her dream of the *huipil* to our circle, I asked everyone who listened to it to wear the dream like one wears a *huipil. (See page 74)* I have, I realize now as we come to a conclusion, been wearing the dream during the time of writing this book. The dream has become part of our council.

Grief and vision. Horror and possibility. The devastation and the Garden. Re-wilding. What we have wrought and what we might save.

The mute crucified man – what does he want to say to us?

༄

I want to know where the weed, hope, grows,
Hardy, indigenous, exactly aligned with place,
A food or habitat or shelter for creatures,

A beacon or sweet for hummingbirds,
Unregulated but companionable,
And faithful, returning year after year,
Rising up and, of course, dying down,
To make way for the next flowering generation,
But certain to return if left alone
In its own place among its own.

c/3

Anguish and Grief. And still we must remember that the rhinos came to greet us, and the test of the Bunker Bomb has been indefinitely postponed. And the Ambassadors came and introduced us to their little ones. Then the Ambassador threw us a bone.

Here then is a last story to sustain us.

A book can be an invocation. It can inform or entertain us, but it can also carry the heart and spirit of what is being discussed. When I wrote *Entering the Ghost River: Meditations on the Theory and Practice of Healing*, I wanted to invoke the spirit of community. Accordingly, we placed one of the Hebrew Holy Letters, *Samach*, ס the circle, the endless cycle, on each page. Then when *Doors: A Fiction for Jazz Horn* was published we placed a *Dalet* ד, door, on each page to open the door to Spirit.

For a long time, I had been wondering what Holy Letter is appropriate for *From Grief Into Vision*. I wanted to place the Holy Letter *Tav*, ת on each page because it is the last letter of the alphabet and includes within it all the other letters and so, I reasoned, it is the letter of council. But, having been so well guided through the ordeal and joy of writing this book, I could not arbitrarily choose a letter but needed to seek the counsel of Spirit.

Accordingly, I sat down with the deck I have of Holy Letters and asked the question, admitting, sheepishly, that I had an opinion and a hope that it would be *Tav* that would be granted to me.

Yes, I was dismayed when the Letter *Lamed* ל leaped out of the deck. But I was quickly chagrined to discover that ל is exactly the right letter for this book for ל means to learn and to teach. It is also a goad or prod for guiding oxen. So *Lamed* indicates a movement toward something. And as it is the first letter of the word *lev*, it stands for the heart.

Lamed signifies a time for initiating action, initiating the movement of action that aligned with our heart, with our innermost desires, with our greatest purposes.[xxxii]

Is this not another way of rendering the hexagram we received at the Nevada Test Site?

Focus on a single idea. Use that to impose a direction on your life. Concentrate everything on this goal.

This is the way I had written about it in *Entering the Ghost River:*

Lamed

Learning and teaching. The teacher and the student stand before the agonies and the mysteries of our time and respond with the wisdom of the heart. The teacher teaches peacemaking and the student becomes a peacemaker. One calls the other into being. The small flame of the moon is a light in the dark night of these times. These are the days when we are learning again and again what the words, "Thou shalt not," mean. The ability to say "No." The willingness to say "No." The heart to say "No." Thou shalt not kill. "No, we will not kill." Thou shalt not steal. Thou shalt not bear false witness. Thou shalt not covet. We agree, "No." No killing. No theft. No coveting. No bearing false witness. Lamed invokes the Lamed Vav, the ones who secretly and tirelessly carry the suffering and righteous action on behalf of the world. Lamed invokes the heart. Lamed invokes the Lamed Vav here. In us. [xxxiii]

Yes, surely this was the right letter and once again Spirit had shown how limited human wisdom and understanding is in the face of the holy.

At the end of the day, however, as I was stepping away from the computer, I saw that there was a Letter on the floor by my feet. When I bent down to turn it over, I saw that it was a *Tav* ת.

Tav completes the Invocation. It is complete. All the Letters are in this last Letter. All the prayers are in this prayer. Stamps, marks, signs, seals. We bear the mark on our foreheads of those who have killed their brothers. Repentance. *Teshuvah.* We do *Teshuvah.* We make amends. We repent. We make reparations. We return to holiness. We follow Torah, the Law. We follow the cosmic law. Prayer. We pray that God will bring Peace to the world. We speak the truth. We live in truth. *Emet* is the seal. *Emet. Tikkun Olam.* We do the work of *Tikkun Olam.* We rectify, we redeem, we repair the world. We live among all beings as equals and so we make the world whole. The world is redeemed. The world is made whole. *Tav* invokes *Tikkun Olam.*[xxxiv]

∾

Here we are. Tikkun Olam. Repair the world. Restore creation. It has been a long journey that has brought us back here to the beginning of possibility and hope.

About Apocalypse. I awaken this morning entirely grateful to Nancy Myers, Carolyn Raffensperger and Lawrie Hartt with whom I have wrestled with the question of apocalypse. This morning I recognize that difficult as it may have been, the ferment between us was necessary. It has led me, blessedly, to the simplest understanding.

Apocalypse implies that the destruction and desecration of the land and world is divinely and spiritually mandated. This is a fallacy, a pernicious lie. This idea is dangerous to all living things.

Rather, the activities that encourage the end of the world, particularly through sowing fear, enacting violence, waging war, degrading the environment, rampantly hunting and killing animals, relentlessly chopping down trees, using up all the resources and despoiling the environment itself, are acts against the Divine.

I cannot find other words for what is insisting itself to be said: The holy intent is for us to cease and desist our destructive activities, and find all the beautiful and sacred ways to sustain the natural world and to restore creation.

I hereby stand with those who refuse the language and intentions of apocalypse.

∽

This morning I came across a line from *The Woman in the Shaman's Body* by Barbara Tedlock. "While shamans are primarily concerned with the maintenance or restoration of equilibrium in individuals, no shaman exists without a culture or subculture to interact with." [xxxv]

Council, writing matrices, the sharing of stories and visions, speaking our dreams, allying with the animals, the elementals, and the ancestors, calling each other forth, and offering ourselves to the spirits that they may use us well, are the ways, also, that we can call such cultures that can and will sustain all beings into being. Everything that we have spoken about here can be understood within the definitions of shamanism but this is not a call to shamanism. It is a most loving and hopeful call to all people and practitioners of healing into collaboration to recover the wisdom that lies within the conversations, alliances and partnerships with all beings on behalf of healing ourselves, our communities, the world. It is a call to heal and sustain and restore creation.

I ask the Vision Quest Tarot for a card with which to end this little book. The card that falls out of the deck is *V, Shaman.*

Be grateful the Shaman is the intuitive who carries the wisdom of Elders. The Shaman reminds us of our spiritual heritage, pointing to the source, the unnameable, the mystery of experience, the power that created everything and absorbs us back into itself at the end of this life." [xxxvi]

∽

Whom do we have to become to carry and bear the gifts given to us?

☙

The future will be taken care of. There will be a future.
We have been charged.

☙

"Many stories have been heard that the sun will go out,
the world will come to an end.
But if we all act well and think well it will not end.
That is why we are still looking after
the sun and the moon and the land."

– The Elder Brothers [xxxvii]

Topanga
5/27/06 10:02 PM

CODA

*H*ere come the broken ones, the holy ones.

The fragment of elephant brain that I was given by Kate Nelson who was given it, in turn, by a Masai warrior, is beside me as I write. It is, itself, breaking apart. Irregular holes have formed that allow one to see through the fragile corrugations of bone to the other side. I am looking through it as into a dream I had so long ago in which layered openings revealed the depth of the sky and I traveled unhampered deep into the sanctity of blue.

What is on the other side of this mind that is gathering and gathering us into it? Whatever I say here about what I see and what I am observing will be insufficient. You will have to gather yourself into the fold. There have never been such times. We cannot know what we are being called to know unless we learn it from within the sacred understanding of the heart.

I sit with a friend from Iraq who has had to flee Baghdad. What is the solution? We do not know the way, but we agree there are ways. Despite the horrific destruction of the war, she knows there are ways. We do not want to demonize anyone. We ask, what has driven all of these people, Americans, Iraqis, Christians, Jews, Muslims, secularists, young and old, men and women, to such violence? What has led us to rape and torture? What has led us to poison the earth? What has made us all terrorists? And what is the way to the blue?

Spirit called me to forty-nine days of silence and solitude this past summer. Forty-nine days so I could shed involvement with the human community, its ideas, assumptions and principles, and listen deeply through the silence to what Spirit might say. "What are the ways to restore creation?" I asked.

I was refused the knowledge of how we might restore creation, but I also came to understand that restoration is possible. As knowledge is power and power is dangerous, I was refused the knowledge. I am grateful for the refusal. I have faith in it.

On the forty-first day, after a day of vision, I learned that my beloved wolf, Akasha, was dying. Though I had committed to staying in solitude for the forty-nine days, a sacred pledge, I drove to Spokane from my retreat cabin at Wolf Creek in British Columbia, left my car at the airport and flew home. Akasha took me and the community into the mourning hut and taught us the rituals of dying. The night I returned, I slept outside in a tent with her, as Valerie Wolf had the night before. When I couldn't sustain the position of embracing her while we were sleeping and withdrew my arm to rest beside her, she touched her paw to my hand and so we spent the night. When she died within the circle of her human community and her companion wolf, Blue, it was as if a spirit had passed through the room and imperceptibly exited. I understand that I had been asked to make a sacrifice on behalf of a wolf.

This book is going to press in a few days. We are involved in the final copyediting. This dawn, I was awakened by the gentlest breath. A young wolf had placed her muzzle against my mouth to indicate that she needed to go outside. Gesture, breath, fur, softness, color, bearing, familiarity all indicated Akasha. But it is Cherokee who has just arrived by plane from Wolf Creek in British Columbia, where I had been in retreat, because she is suddenly homeless. Her presence is a great mystery. I understand that I had been asked to make a sacrifice, taking her on in a very difficult time, on behalf of a wolf. It is possible that Cherokee is pregnant. If so, she will whelp the puppies in the secret garden that is outside our bedroom window, the site where Akasha is buried and where her spirit abides.

After Akasha's death, I went into silence again for seven days. How shall I summarize the time?

Perhaps in this way: Let us speak the stories of the presence of Spirit to each other. Let us become vessels for Spirit to act through, each one of us discerning the path we are called to for the sake of creation. How shall we restore creation? By restoring the natural world. Restore creation by restoring creation. How simple. And finally, "Teach Beauty." And, again; how simple.

Naba Al Barrak and I come to the understanding that we cannot continue the course of designating right and wrong, friends and enemies, us and them. Naba says that every Iraqi remembers when Saddam Hussein threatened that anyone who opposed him would reap only skulls and sand. His curse is coming to be. Skulls and sand echo in my mind like the Yale fraternity initiations of desecration, President George W. Bush and his father and grandfather before him, participated in, Skull and Bones. The curse also has equally terrible resonance with Shock and Awe.

Listening to an ex-U.S. military commander denounce Shock and Awe as inappropriate, that is, as inefficient war tactics, I am horrified by what we have become. We no longer question the assumption that there should be, that we should be a world power. We do not question the idea of domination; we ask only the immoral question: How shall we achieve it at the least cost to ourselves? We do not see that those, including ourselves, who torture and destroy, create the terrorists who will rise up against us, and in turn, inspire more terrorism, individual or governmental, violence and rage.

We must all take responsibility for who we have become, for how humans have devastated the world, are ravaging the natural world, are torturing animals, for how we kill, choose violence, valorize defense, revere weapons and transform the gods of love into gods of war, Aphrodite to Aries, Yahweh, Jesus and Allah to Moloch. Each of us has acted against the teachings of our heart, has acted against our soul. It is time to bear witness to our shame, to stand undefended against our singular and collective grief. When we do this we will know how to proceed. Though his memoir, *Beim Häuten der Zwiebel* is not released yet in English, and so I haven't read it, I imagine Günter Grass is engaging in the kind of reflection that all of us, citizens, soldiers, veterans, intellectuals, political activists, religious leaders, politicians, human beings are being required to enter. Who will stand with us to examine our souls?

છ૭

everyday gandhis called a council in early October that included participants from Liberia, Ivory Coast, Ghana, Sierra Leone and Guinea, as well as from the U.S.. History, circumstances and vision have been changing the focus of **everyday gandhis** in the last few years. It has developed from an NGO documenting and supporting grassroots peacebuilding activities to an NGO that has envisioned mourning feasts and other traditional wisdom ways of peacebuilding. In a council in 2005, William Saa announced that he had been called to seek out the ones who had killed his brother during the war to enter into a process of reconciliation with them. "As my brother is dead," he said, "I will ask them to be my brothers." Afterwards, he returned to Liberia to find, dig up and rebury the remains of his brother. In doing so, he learned the particulars of his brother's death. It had been on hearing of his brother's death while starving and in hiding in Monrovia from the various killing rampages from all sides that were devastating Liberia, that Bill saw that he had only two choices – to become a revengeful killer or to become a peacebuilder. Obviously, he chose the latter and became a nationally recognized trauma expert and trainer before joining **everyday gandhis**: "In Africa, if I am healed, I can heal 20 people just by interacting with them. They each can heal 20 people, who in turn, heal 20 people. That's how it works."

Now, while supporting this profound and most personal work of reconciliation, we were sitting before the daunting realization that peacebuilding is intrinsically connected with restoration, the restoration of the natural world.

> The question at the core of **everyday gandhis** is: What is the story of how lasting peace is created? With deep gratitude, **everyday gandhis** offers stories of peacebuilding in the words of those who have known war and violence. Through dreams and indigenous traditions, we honor the living, the ancestors and all of Creation. May the experience of receiving these stories be as healing as the process of telling them and being heard. May they awaken and sustain the peacemaker within us. May words and images of peace become the new reality of our time and times to come.
>
> **everyday gandhis** Mission Statement

After ten days, we understood the true blessing of council and took on the mandate of further forging alliances with traditional wisdom ways in order to restore the wild in Liberia and other West African countries as essential activities of peacebuilding. We began to imagine the redemption, rehabilitation and education of ex-combatants and child soldiers as part of sustainable processes establishing and restoring parks and sanctuaries for the land and sea animals, for the water and the forests. In council, we saw how essential it is to incorporate the traditional wisdom ways in any planning or development for it is here that the deep knowledge of cohabitation lies and it is through this knowledge that the guidance and assistance of the spirits can be realized. If we had not sat in council for so many days, we would not have fully understood this.§

While we were meeting, we learned that a small group of elephants had returned to the Voinjama area in Lofa county in Liberia. There are many stories about their return, including that the oldest elephant died, that the body was distributed to a village for food and that one of the tusks was taken by poachers. We heard that the villagers are alarmed and the government would like the elephants to return to the forest because the elephants have eaten pumpkin and corn crops; the dry season is coming and so is the inevitable food scarcity. We still do not know if there is food for the elephants in the neighboring forests, or what the effect of the dry season will be for them, or whether they will be safe from poachers, villagers, and the ex-combatants who may also have no place to live other than the forest. One of the stories is that now that peace is returning, the elephants are "repatriating" from neighboring Guinea whose savannas are not the ideal habitat for them. It was suggested that the renewed spiritual environment in Voinjama calls to them because of the benevolent consequences of the mourning feasts of reconciliation that **everyday gandhis** originated and sponsored.

Because we were speaking of elephants, I gave a copy of Jami Sieber's CD "Hidden Sky" to Bill Saa. I didn't know why he looked so astonished; it was because he was leaving immediately after the council to spend a week offering training in Thailand on trauma healing. He had not known about the Elephant Orchestra. Returning from Thailand, he said the high point of his trip was visiting a rehabilitation site for elephants where they paint and make music. He stood close to the elephants there and felt great love and connection emanating from them to him.

Dreams, journeys, consultations with governmental and environmental organizations, as well as consultations with *zoes* and spiritual

---

§ *The proceedings of this council that included Liberians, West Africans, representatives from SEHN and Liberia's environmental organization, and participants from various Daré's will eventually be posted and distributed by **everyday gandhis**. Check their website in 2007 for them.*

leaders informed our council deliberations. One Liberian *zo* dreamed that a herd of elephants was carrying peacebuilders to a conference to reconcile two embattled villages that would have been cancelled because of transportation difficulties.

Cynthia Travis dreamed that Christian Bethelson was leading a V-shaped phalanx of people toward a V-shaped phalanx of elephants. Bethelson and the lead elephant met where the two V's converged and bowed down to each other. Why were the elephants willing to meet with Bethelson? she asked in the dream. Because if we can trust him, we can trust anyone, they answered. As if following the commentary implicit to the dream, Bethelson has been speaking to ex-combatants about the transformation from being soldiers to becoming guardians for the elephants and the wild. In terms of bringing healing to the ex-combatants themselves, much Bethelson's concern, Danelia Wild has posed this question: Has anyone worked to heal the ex-combatants by consulting their dreams? Ed Tick, also the author of *The Practice of Dream Healing*, based on the ancient Greek Asklepian tradition would say, "Yes", affirmatively. In Liberia, we will see what possibilities this offers when we return to meet both elephants and ex-combatants in February, 2007.

৩

My own deliberations had led me to understand how disturbed the elephants are at losing habitat and culture. Loss of culture and social cohesiveness is a consequence of the elders and matriarchs being hunted for their tusks. Rampage is an inevitable consequence of these circumstances among animals as it is among humans. The Liberian *zoes* informed us that the traditional ceremonies and sacrifices that were regularly offered on behalf of right relationship between the people and the elephants had been interrupted and had not, because of economic exigencies and the imposition of western, imperial scientific, rational and religious mind sets, been resumed after the war. So the cultures between and among the people and the elephants had also been interrupted. Restoration had to consider all of this: economics, land, culture and Spirit.

It was Elenna Rubin Goodman who saw that the villagers who had eaten the oldest elephant could, through the rite of transubstantiation, be receiving the wisdom of the elephant ancestor. All of this auguring possibilities for peace between human and non-human species but only when consciously honored. **everyday gandhis** searched for the ways and means to support the resumption of the traditional ceremonies while I urged that the bones of the oldest elephant be made available to the elephants, either where the death occurred or in a protected place agreeable to both species, so the elephants could engage in their mourning rituals. I saw there was a blessed parallel between the human mourning feast rituals and the elephant mourning rituals and the possibilities of peace, reconciliation and restoration.

The words I heard were clear: Even the elephants cannot endure separation from their culture and their land. Such separations have made humans violent and are driving elephants mad. If the elephants have access to the bones of their dead, they will heal. If the people recognize this and also restore their own appropriate traditional ritual ways, the elephants will return to their old ways of co-existence. If people persist in living only within the most limited modern understandings and activities, more and more elephants will be damaged and will act accordingly. More and more violence will occur as they are deprived of the old wisdom and the security of the land. This is a world-wide situation.

Consulting the I Ching oracle, I was/we were confirmed and unnerved by the specific commentary contained in Hexagram 16, Providing For/Riding the Elephant. The designated changing lines stated:

"Don't be skeptical about this connection and don't hold back. This is real. Doubting and equivocating will only bring you sorrow. Provide what is needed, simply and directly.

"A great purpose is moving here. This undertaking is sent from heaven. It gives you everything you need. Have no doubts. Partners join together in this."

Today, November 19, 2006, Cynthia Travis informs me that five different ceremonies will be performed to heal the breach between the people and the elephants and that one of the **everyday gandhis** team in Liberia has walked from village to village speaking to the inhabitants, *zoes*, elders, and elephant totem people about the situation. One of the ceremonies arranged is where the community asks the ancestors to speak to the elephants to find out what they want.

Liberia is not the only country, however, to witness elephants entering into village and agricultural areas at this time. Elephants seeking out their original habitats and migration routes have entered human

populated areas all over Asia and Africa where they have been designated as "rogue" or "rampaging." In council, we found ourselves recognizing and confronting the elephants' spiritual presence and their rage
as we followed the news of their simultaneous appearances worldwide.

In Botswana, Cynthia Travis had wondered whether the elephants
who came to meet us were in communication with the elephants in
Liberia who had been so overwhelmed, like the rest of the wildlife, by
the war and the resulting economic and social ruin. As if echoing the
recent I Ching reading, she had asked then, "Why would we deny it?"
as miracle upon miracle confirmed its possibility. Now, we had confir-
mations as startling as the ways in which the elephants had called us to
them originally, communicating with us across geographic and species
lines.

While we were contemplating in council the daunting concerns before us, we came upon the remarkable cover article in the *New York Times*
Magazine, October 7, 2006, "An Elephant Crackup?" by Charles Seibert.§
Herein, Seibert chronicles increasing incidents of elephant violence, ag-
gression and even perversion. "In the past 12 years, elephants have killed
605 people in Assam, India ... In northeastern India, 265 elephants have
died in that same period, the majority of them as a result of retaliation
by angry villagers." Citing such events of violence and counter-violence
globally, he continues that young male elephants in parks and game reserves in South Africa "have been raping and killing rhinoceroses."

I think immediately of our invasion of Iraq, of Abu Ghraib and

---

§ *The entire article, no longer available free on the New York Times website,
can be read in its entirety on the website of the Elephant Sanctuary*
http://www.elephants.com/ *in Tennessee which describes itself this way: "The
Elephant Sanctuary in Hohenwald, Tennessee, is the nation's largest natural-
habitat refuge developed specifically to meet the needs of endangered elephants. It
is a non-profit organization, licensed by the U.S. Department of Agriculture and
the Tennessee Wildlife Resources Agency, designed specifically for old, sick or needy
elephants who have been retired from zoos and circuses. Utilizing more than 2700
acres, it provides three separate and protected, natural-habitat environments for
Asian and African elephants. Our residents are not required to perform or entertain for the public; instead, they are encouraged to live like elephants."*

*Visitors to the Sanctuary cannot observe the elephants so that they can live
their lives as close as possible to what they would have in earlier times enjoyed in
the wild, but an elephant cam is available on the net.*

Guantanamo.   What causes American soldiers to commit atrocities is
not yet clear though many of us are thinking it has to do with the separation from the natural world, the loss of true elders, the public corruption of values, and the true madness of replacing wisdom traditions
and rituals with media events and entertainments that center upon
mindless violence. If we do not yet know about our own, if we have not
faced our own collusion in a tragic, lethal and violent culture, we do
know of the now world-wide and horrifically common practices of forcing people to observe family members tortured, raped and killed, or of
kidnapping children or young people, drugging them, forcing them to
kill a member of their family and thereby creating an enduring killer
through such activities. These activities bear alarming similarities to the
plight of elephants.

Seibert writes that many assaults on the rhinos were caused by
young males who not only witnessed their families shot down in culls
but were tethered to the dead and dying relatives until they were
rounded up to be transported to other locations. It has become stan-
dard to replace this barbarian practice by culling the entire herd so that
there are no survivors to remember. However, it has been found that
elephants do communicate across vast distances, far vaster than the
sound waves can travel, and so the news of the culls are transmitted and
so we cannot avoid the consequences of slaughter.

Trying to understand this phenomenon with fresh intelligence,
Seibert interviewed Gay Bradshaw and Eve Abe who are collaborating
in establishing a sanctuary in Uganda for the treatment of elephants and
humans suffering from post traumatic stress disorder.§

Seibert quotes Gay Bradshaw: "In 'Elephant Breakdown,' a 2005
essay in the journal *Nature*, Bradshaw and several colleagues argued that
today's elephant populations are suffering from a form of chronic stress,
a kind of species-wide trauma. Decades of poaching and culling and
habitat loss, they claim, have so disrupted the intricate web of familial
and societal relations by which young elephants have traditionally been

---

§ *Another synchronistic circumstance – our **everyday gandhis** council would
end with a healing music daré offered to Ba-foday Suma, a member of **everyday
gandhis**, a European trained economist as well as a Muslim and traditional elder
from Guinea and Sierra Leone. Joining us would be my husband and Ed Tick
on their return that day from a journey of forgiveness and reconciliation to Vietnam in the company of several American veterans.*

raised in the wild, and by which established elephant herds are governed, that what we are now witnessing is nothing less than a precipitous collapse of elephant culture." Later in the article he makes a statement that is a decided echo of what I tried to convey in "Mandlovu Mind"[§]:

"Elephants, when left to their own devices, are profoundly social creatures. A herd of them is, in essence, one incomprehensibly massive elephant: a somewhat loosely bound and yet intricately interconnected, tensile organism."

Siebert also detailed elephants' involvement in mourning rituals. "When an elephant dies, its family members engage in intense mourning and burial rituals, conducting weeklong vigils over the body, carefully covering it with earth and brush, revisiting the bones for years afterward, caressing the bones with their trunks." Similar, again, to what I had written in *Entering the Ghost River* and elsewhere, it served to have this documented in the *New York Times*. Citing the article, I was able, within a few days of its publication, to write to a newspaper in Ranji, India regarding elephants that were disturbing a village having sensed that one of their herd had died. The elephant, the villagers said, had drowned in an irrigation ditch and they had buried her. I advised the terrified villagers to exhume the body of the elephant and leave it in a suitable place so that the elephants might enter into the ritual that would ease them. I do not know whether my letter reached the villagers or whether the editors of the newspaper printed it after it was translated into Hindi, but it was deeply gratifying to be able to advise them on behalf of the elephants with the backing of an article in a most respectable but conventional newspaper. The mysterious and unfathomable has entered the common discourse.

In a conversation that followed between Gay Bradshaw and myself, she confirmed Seibert's statements, that in consultation with such luminary African-elephant researchers as Daphne Sheldrick, Joyce Poole and Cynthia Moss, as well as researchers in human neuroscience, she had come to understand elephant behavior in terms of trauma. We agreed with each other's understandings that the same conditions caused the same trauma and aberrant behavior in elephants, and other non-human species, as they caused in humans and that, as a corollary,

---

[§] *See "Mandlovu Mind," page 128.*

similar interventions or restorations offered all species the possibility of healing.

I wrote to Eve Abe, colleague and collaborator of Gay Bradshaw: "I sense that we are all in an amazing alliance and collaboration on behalf of restoration of the traditional wisdom traditions, the souls of soldiers, children and everyone devastated by war and colonialism, and the parallel restoration of the souls and lives of the animals and of the natural world." Eve Abe is a London-based animal ethologist since visa difficulties prevent her from returning to Uganda where her work is located. According to Seibert: "She received her doctorate at Cambridge University in 1994 for work detailing the parallels she saw between the plight of Uganda's orphaned male elephants and the young male orphans of her own people, the Acholi, whose families and villages have been decimated by years of civil war."

ℰℛ

It all comes together. Such is the nature of vision. It is a story, a complex response to a complex set of circumstances. We are all in the story of the ways devastation can become restoration. In a follow-up letter to the October council I wrote, "It is clear to me that we are in a ferment of possibility that includes the storytelling, peacebuilding restoration work of **everyday gandhis**, the environmental work of Liberia's SANFU, Save My Future Foundation, SEHN's work with the Precautionary Principle, the Commons and Guardianship as outlined in the Bemidji Statement, Ed Tick's work restoring soul and healing PTSD in veterans and ex-combatants, and the amazing work and understanding carried by Eve Abe and Gay Bradshaw. Profound cultural and systemic changes are implicit here through the restoration of the natural world and the traditional wisdom traditions. How similar our thinking is ... I cannot help but believe that the elephants are teaching us. I believe we are involved in working alliances that will help us transform ourselves and ex-combatants to become guardians, support the elephants in their mourning rituals, sustain elders in their commitment to the wisdom of their traditions and so begin the work of restoration on all levels. All these as essential activities of peacebuilding. A mandate of restoration has been given to us. Hope and possibility are emerging from visions that coexist among us."

On a teaching tour on the east coast, I met a Christian minister who said she had dreamed of rhinoceroses and wooly mammoths breaking into the walls of her house. Over time these dreams revealed she has Lyme disease, long before doctors could make the diagnosis. When medicine confirmed her understanding, it was too late; the illness had caused brain damage. As a consequence, she has remained devoted to her dreams and is mapping her brain, based on the information they are giving to her, information, she says that is being corroborated by the latest scientific research. "You know," she said with great seriousness, "the brain is a council."

I read these final words to Michael who says, "I am suddenly in a herd of elephants that happen to be ideas." Mandlovu mind. Elephant totem. Alliance.

War-torn, impoverished, crazed, disoriented, homeless, orphaned, terrified, hungry – these are the broken ones whose anguish is signaling to us over vast distances and seemingly impenetrable barriers, to gather in councils, to restore the old wisdom ways, to restore the land, to cross the species lines, to rely on the guidance and teachings of Spirit.

Let us face what we have done and, in doing so, let us become vessels fitting for Spirit to act through us. Here we come, the broken ones, the holy ones, to restore creation, from grief into vision.

ॐ

APPENDICES

CHERNOBYL: PROMETHEUS UNBOUND

By Stephan David Hewitt

*I*n the center of town in the city of Pripyat, Ukraine, there stood a statue of Prometheus stealing fire from the Gods. It was a symbol of the superiority of human endeavor in this modern city that was built a few miles away from a four nuclear power plant complex. Built in the early 1970s for the workers and their families, Pripyat had all the modern conveniences – a cultural center, music hall, modern high rise apartment buildings, several athletic stadiums. Russia's nuclear power plant next door had a flawless safety record; it was the model of technological prowess. It was the showcase city of its day, set in a beautiful countryside on a river, its population increasing each year.

On April 26, 1986 in a routine test of safety procedures, one of the four nuclear reactors at Chernobyl overheated and exploded in the early hours of the morning, releasing 400 times the amount of radioactivity of Hiroshima and Nagasaki's atomic bombs in a massive plume that shot deadly radioactive particles several miles high into the sky. The city of Pripyat slept peacefully unaware of what had happened. The next day, readings jumped from 15,000 times normal to 600,000 times normal radiation level, while children still played in the streets and life continued unaware of the horror of what had happened in the night. Such levels of radioactivity in nature had never been measured before. The men taking the readings wondered if their Geiger counters were working properly. Though no one was told the truth about what had happened, people knew from the workers that there had been an explosion at the plant, and must have found it suspect that there were troops of police walking through the streets with gas masks on. No one knew that the metallic taste in everyone's mouths was radioactive iodine from nuclear fallout.

Elena Filatova: I travel a lot and one of my favorite destinations leads North from Kiev, towards so called Chernobyl "dead zone" which is 130 kms from my home. Why my favorite? Because one can take long rides there on empty roads. The people there all left and nature is blooming. There are beautiful woods and lakes. In places where roads have not been traveled by trucks or army vehicles, they are in the same condition they were 20 years ago - except for an occasional blade of grass or some tree that discovered a crack to spring through. Time does not ruin roads, so they may stay this way until they can be opened to normal traffic again........ a few centuries from now. ... On the Friday evening of April 25, 1986, the reactor crew at Chernobyl-4, prepared to run a test the next day to see how long the turbines would keep spinning and producing power if the electrical power supply went off line. This was a dangerous test, but it had been done before. As a part of the preparation, they disabled some critical control systems — including the automatic shutdown safety mechanisms.

Shortly after 1:00 AM on April 26, the flow of coolant water dropped and the power began to increase.

At 1:23 AM, the operator moved to shut down the reactor in its low power mode and a domino effect of previous errors caused an sharp power surge, triggering a tremendous steam explosion which blew the 1000 ton cap on the nuclear containment vessel to smithereens.

Some of the 211 control rods melted and then a second explosion, whose cause is still the subject of disagreement among experts, threw out fragments of the burning radioactive fuel core and allowed air to rush in — igniting several tons of graphite insulating blocks.

Once graphite starts to burn, it's almost impossible to extinguish. It took 9 days and 5000 tons of sand, boron, dolomite, clay and lead dropped from helicopters to put it out. The radiation was so intense that many of those brave pilots died.

It was this graphite fire that released most of the radiation into the atmosphere and troubling spikes in atmospheric radiation were measured as far away as Sweden — thousands of miles away.

The causes of the accident are described as a fateful combination of human error and imperfect technology.

In keeping with a long tradition of Soviet justice, they imprisoned all the people who worked on that shift — regardless of their guilt. The man who tried to stop the chain reaction in a last desperate attempt to avoid the meltdown was sentenced to 14 years in prison. He died 3 weeks later.

Radiation will stay in the Chernobyl area for the next 48,000 years, but humans may begin repopulating the area in about 600 years — give or take three centuries.

http://www.kiddofspeed.com/chapter1.html.

Rumors grew rapidly that something was terribly wrong, and fear and panic mounted. From the tops of the apartment buildings, one could see that the roof of one of the reactors was no longer there, and a horrifyingly strange yellow-green glow emanated from the exposed smoking hole. Since wood absorbs radioactivity rapidly, the trees around the plant were glowing red.

A day and a half later, buses began to pour into Pripyat to evacuate the entire city of 47,000 people. They were all told they would return in 3 days, and were given 2 hours, under gunpoint, to assemble their belongings and leave. No one has ever returned to Pripyat to live, or to any of the surrounding villages in that region. One older man who stayed behind was found dead a few weeks later. No one was allowed to take their pets, which, days later, roamed in packs. Soldiers were sent in to destroy them.

A "Dead Zone" of over eleven hundred square miles now surrounds the Chernobyl plant. Belarus, just north of Ukraine, suffered the greatest permanent damage, as most of the deadly radioactive fallout landed there in the first days after the explosion. Elena Filatova reports that ninety-nine percent of Belarus is contaminated. Twenty years later, it is still dangerous to stand next to the fire trucks that first responded to the explosion. Most all of the firefighters who responded to the blaze have since died, including one for whom April 26th was to be his wedding day. There are now fields as far as the eye can see of vehicles that were used in the cleanup, abandoned and cordoned off with radiation warning signs because they are so contaminated. In the days following the disaster, more than 140,000 people were moved out of the zone around the Chernobyl plant. They were bussed to various cities and towns, dispersed quickly, often with no regard for family ties. Some children were separated from their mothers; some fathers who worked at the plant and were hospitalized for radiation sickness, never returned to their families, and no word was sent. There was a panic of war in the air, though the killer, radiation, was invisible.

The aftermath of the explosion of Chernobyl goes on and on. Seventy whole villages were flattened and buried because of extreme contamination. More continue to be razed each year. Children born now, twenty years later, are showing increased cancer levels, deformities and other horrors of radiation poisoning. No one knows, as statistics have never been released, how many lives have been tragically altered from the incident. Over 600,000 people were involved in the cleanup and no data exists pertaining to their health. What does exist now that did not exist before Chernobyl are many homes for abandoned babies that are full of the most pitiful creatures, babies born with spinal deformities, grossly misshapen limbs and/or severe mental retardation. They are overcrowded and money for them is limited. In Belarus alone the infant mortality rate is 300 percent higher than the rest of Europe. In Ukraine, there is a condition known as "Chernobyl Heart" which describes the all-too common condition of children who are born with holes in the walls of their hearts.[1] Money for the operations needed to repair these hearts is not available. Sometimes operations are donated by volunteer doctors through organizations such as the International Children's Heart Foundation,[2] and while one volunteer doctor working overtime may do 13 open heart surgeries in a visit, still there are hundreds of children who are placed on the waiting list that will die within 2 to 5 years.

In the weeks following the Chernobyl disaster, Russia was forced to seek help from the outside world. They were in over their heads and they knew it. Panic ensued with the realization that the molten core still burning in the reactor could break through the containment floor and contact the water table beneath. (Chernobyl is set near the Pripyat River, now utterly contaminated). If this should happen, a second explosion so

---

[1] *There is also a film "Chernobyl Heart" which won the Oscar for Best Documentary Short Subject in 2004.*

See http://www.ccp-intl.org/chernobyl_heart.html *for more info.*

[2] http://www.babyhearts.com/introduction.php

near to the other three nuclear plants would spread tons of plutonium and other radioactive materials over all of Europe, making it uninhabitable for centuries. (Plutonium, by the way, is a man-made substance, not occurring naturally on the planet, except in trace amounts; it is the stuff nuclear bombs are made of.) One microgram of plutonium can be lethal for human beings. There is enough plutonium inside of Chernobyl to kill one hundred million people. According to Dr. John W. Gofman, the co-discoverer of uranium-233, three tablespoons of it can produce cancer in half a billion people.[3] Every nuclear power plant produces about 30 tons of nuclear waste each year of its operation.[4] Weapons grade plutonium has a half-life of about 24,000 years, while another kind of plutonium decays into americium, an element that has an even stronger and more dangerous radiation output.

Consultants from the International Atomic Energy Commission were brought to the site, and plans were made to build a thick concrete slab which then was placed under the melted core to prevent it from devastating contact with the water table. Then a "sarcophagus" of steel and concrete walls 20 feet thick was rapidly constructed to keep the contaminants inside from being further spread to the environment[5]. This sarcophagus, however, is extremely dangerous today; it is leaking, and it rests upon the walls of the original containment building, which were blown sideways and could collapse at any time. And the covering is by no means airtight. There are large holes in it, some large enough to drive a car through, which were intentionally made to let the heat escape. Birds fly in and out, and when it rains the leaking roof lets out a nightmare of dangerous particles. The tons of dust inside the sarcophagus are a major problem; if it should collapse, there would be another environmental disaster, adding to the already overwhelming impact Chernobyl has had upon the people and the land. Plans are now underway to use international funds to build another sarcophagus at a cost of US$1 billion.

---

[3] The People's Almanac, ©1975, David Wallace & Irving Wallace, Doubleday & Co., Inc.

[4] http://library.thinkquest.org/3471/nuclear_waste_body.html

[5] *The extensive damage to the environment caused by the explosion released only 3-5% of the radioactive materials in the reactor. The rest is still under the sarcophagus.*

What business do we have constructing power plants that have the capability of such devastation? It is all about business, actually. Only one ounce of uranium when fissioned in a reactor provides the energy equivalent of burning 100 tons of coal. Large corporate profits can be made from nuclear power, but only if the nuclear industry is not held accountable for the ramifications of the serious environmental impacts. The clean-up costs of Chernobyl's debacle have so far run over US$18 billion. Total spending by Belarus alone on Chernobyl between 1991 and 2003 is estimated at more than US$13 billion.[6] The numbers of lives lost and affected by the disaster remain shrouded in secrecy. Though critics say the design of the Russian nuclear plants was inherently flawed, no one can deny that every nuclear power plant is capable of creating massive amounts of deadly poisonous spent reactor fuel, and if human error is serious enough, another explosion like Chernobyl.

The effects upon the Russian environment and infant mortality rate have been devastating. The adult mortality rate there has risen alarmingly in the last 20 years, and the average life expectancy for men is now 59 in the former Soviet Union.[7] A U.S. study shows that infant mortality rates decline rapidly in areas where nuclear power plants are closed, by as much as 54 percent in some cases.[8] Mikhail Gorbachev has been campaigning recently on behalf of the environment. He implored London's House of Parliament to, "Think again, think seven times again before you leap and start construction of new nuclear power plants."[9] He knows full well how such a dangerous technology can wreak havoc on an entire nation.

What is the larger story here, and how can we make meaning of Chernobyl in our lives? How do we live, knowing such a shattering disaster has taken place? Astrology as a system of metaphor and archetype may have a few answers. Pluto, the planetary body, was discovered in 1930, and its archetypal symbology is the dominant theme of the 20th

---

[6] *The Chernobyl Forum: 2003-2005, Second revised version,* www.iaea.org. *Published by the Int'l Atomic Energy Agency in Austria, April 2006, p.33*

[7] *ibid, Chernobyl Forum., p. 35*

[8] http://www.mothersalert.org/infant.html

[9] *Reuters, "Gorbachev Warns Against New Nuclear Power Plants," June 8, 2006:* http://today.reuters.com/News/CrisesArticle.aspx?storyId=L08375445

[10] *See Tarnas, Richard,* Cosmos and Psyche, *2006, Penguin Group, p. 98 for an exquisite description of Pluto's symbology.*

century and modern industrial civilization.[10] Pluto in astrological symbology represents the force of underworld elemental power that has the potential for deep transformation, the kind of transformation that is, however, phoenix-like. Pluto strips us of all our learned behaviors; it leaves us in touch with our soul's urges for power. This kind of power is large-scale, and thus rules corporate leadership, fascistic dictators, and power-mongering, the kind that the 20th century has infamously fostered, to the great detriment of individuals and personal freedom. As Pluto's power intensifies everything it touches, it brings out the pure, primordial potent, all-consuming force within all of us, bringing us to our knees. If we do not become conscious, it will leave us there.

Pluto also rules deep crisis. We have all experienced at one time or another a death-like situation, whether through a car accident, ill health, job loss or a close personal relationship that dissolves and takes our former life with it. No one can avoid such crises, but if we can find meaning in them, if we can glean from them teachings that make us stronger, we can then pick up the pieces of our former lives and begin anew. In many cases, we could not be who we are now if not for these crises. This is the power of Pluto to transform us. Pluto actually is the bringer of light, the light that shines from the "other side" the immortal inner planes of our existence, wherein lie those deep spiritual truths about ourselves. We cannot see that light because we are mortals; to our human eyes that place looks like blackness, void, and death. It is invisible to us and yet we are deeply affected by it in ways that are largely unconscious.

Radiation too is invisible, and affects us in ways we are only beginning to understand. Certainly, too much of it alters genetic patterns, makes cells go awry and forget they are a part of a larger organism, growing in ways that threaten the health of the body. Cancer, as Deena Metzger has pointed out, is not just an individual disease, but a disease of the entire culture we live in. The sighting of Pluto heralded a new chapter which brought to the surface our relationship to power, to how we perceive ourselves, and this amplification has pushed us to become more blatantly what we are, to the point where we question the very belief systems that underlie our collective world view. What are the ways we do business on this planet that are "cancerous," i.e. that are not congruent with the health of the whole community? Where does competition override cooperation?

Pluto's greatest power is transpersonal and non-egoic, and yet when the ego tries to use this power for its own personal gratification and aggrandizement, when it loses touch with the greater truth, the larger picture, then it becomes destructive, resulting in megalomania, and arrogance of great proportions. Similar to the cancer cell, when we over-identify with being autonomously powerful, we risk great harm to ourselves and our environment. Pluto's penalty for such abuse of its power is often devastating.

As a race of beings, humanity is still in its infancy. Compared to the dinosaurs who lived on this planet for 200 million years, humanity has been around at most for two million years. In that scale of maturity, we are only one year old. Yet we have been given a forebrain with which we can reason, imagine, make pictures and figure things out. We've been given amazing tools, our opposable thumbs, and our minds with which to shape the world around us. We are so enamored of our prowess that we have become arrogant, self-important, believing it is our purpose to dominate and control Nature and the forces that create life on this planet. Whoops!

Out of this arrogance has come the technological age. There have been great benefits from our abilities to serve ourselves with water, electricity and all the accompanying gadgetry of computers and moving information through great channels of intercommunication via the Internet. What miracles have we wrought! And yet, because of this arrogance, we have forgotten what our Native American relatives tried to teach us about respect for the land, for the earth, and for the Great Mother who gives us all these gifts. It is as though we are teenagers who run happily out the door of our native homes, dancing blithely through the land of plenty, consuming all we want, throwing garbage into the river that contains our drinking water, with little thought to the pattern and cycle of life itself.

What we've yet to learn to integrate into our governing systems is the concept of stewardship, of taking care of ourselves and our planet so that we all can live together with some degree of harmony and less harm to each other and the animals, plants and environment. In our craze to develop our rational and thinking minds, we have neglected to develop an equal power of our hearts to love and heal ourselves and the earth around us. The arts and all forms of creativity get us in touch with this power. The deepening of the heart's wisdom reveals to us that we are all connected; the evidence of so much overwhelming sorrow in this post-Chernobyl, post-modern world reminds us to keep our hearts open to forming communities that can help us hold this sorrow, and offer us solutions through mutual assistance.

As humanity emerges from its adolescence and is forced to consider the results of our past transgressions, we are confronting certain knowledge of our potential to destroy our species, and the millions of other species who live on this planet. Gorbachev, realizing the destructive power of Chernobyl, decided a year and a half later to disarm the long-range nuclear warheads Russia had, specifically the SS-18, one missile of which was as powerful as 100 Chernobyls. And they had 2,700 of those missiles! "Imagine the destruction!" Gorbachev said.[11]

If anything, the events of Chernobyl are calling us to face our responsibility to future generations; the new sarcophagus that must be built to contain those still-hot toxic poisons must last longer than the Pyramids if we are to guarantee that life still exists for humankind and all beings. Nuclear wastes, for which there is no fool-proof manner of disposal, must also be guarded carefully for generations to come, as an eventual reminder to future generations of our short-sighted vision.

Sweden was the first country to recognize that the Chernobyl fallout had contaminated its soil, and sounded the alarm to the rest of the world. Shortly after the 1979 Three Mile Island meltdown, Sweden voted to close all nuclear power plants in their country, though they have yet only closed two of their ten reactors in service.[12] Some European countries, including Austria, Italy and Greece have no operating reactors, and Germany has voted to close all its reactors by 2020. But politics continues to shift and intervene, and these decisions are often reversed.

If we are to have a future, we cannot continue the abuse of power by the few to control the many; there must be councils and peacemaking and explorations of ways in which we can use our resources to promote health and safety, and to resist fear-mongering in our own personal

---

[11] *"Battle of Chernobyl"*, *Discovery Channel, 2006*

[12] *BBC News, 1 June, 2005,* http://news.bbc.co.uk/1/hi/sci/tech/4597589.stm *And in recent news, on July 25, 2006, Sweden had an accident at its Forsmark plant that was termed "close to meltdown" and has temporarily closed five of its nuclear reactors as a result.*

lives, as well as in our public arts and politics. There is much to fear, and yet there is much to learn about loving and opening our hearts to the effects of the abuse of our personal power. If we stare at our shadow despite our fear, it can no longer control us. To paraphrase Carl Jung: What we refuse to make conscious, appears in our lives as Fate.

"Imagine the destruction!" Gorbachev said.

Somewhere in the many possible futures that exist in the eleven odd dimensions that we occupy, there is a future in which we are not devastated by nuclear holocaust and environmental disaster.

Pluto is here. Plutonian fate has entered our lives. We can make conscious that which is most difficult and complex. If we are willing, it can forever transform and empower us and lead us toward that future.

ɛ͗ʒ

Ten Tenets:
The Law of the Commons
of the Natural World

By Carolyn Raffensperger

*W*hat is government for? It is to protect the commons, all the things we own together and none of us owns individually, such as air, water, wildlife, the human gene pool, the accumulated human knowledge that we each inherit at birth, and more. Can protecting the commons be expressed in a simple set of guidelines? Here's a start...

The commons (onthecommons.org) includes all the things we own together and none of us owns individually – the air and waters of the Earth, wildlife, the human gene pool, the accumulated human knowledge that we all inherit at birth, and so on. The commons form the biological platform upon which the entire human enterprise – and, indeed, all life – depend.

At present, American law tends to emphasize and give privilege to corporate rights and private property to the exclusion of community, other creatures, health, and future generations. However, hidden like treasure in the depths of our legal system is the foundation of a law of the commons. Some legal precepts derived from ancient practices of people sharing water, land and wildlife still reverberate throughout American law.

One of the oldest ideas, the public trust doctrine, predates the Magna Carta but it is still part of the common law in most of the 50 U.S. states. The public trust doctrine stands for the principle that a government body holds some resource like tidal waters or shores in trust for the people. Versions of this concept have appeared in state constitutions and been adjudicated in state and federal courts.

I have taken these (and other ideas) and distilled ten tenets of commons law on which we might build a more satisfying, coherent law and policy so that we can pass this beautiful world on to future generations.

Ten Tenets: The Law of the Commons of the Natural World

1) The commons shall be passed on to future generations unimpaired.

2) All commoners have equal access to the commons and use by commoners will be allocated without discrimination.

3) Government's key responsibility is to serve as a trustee of the commons. The trust beneficiary is present and future generations. The trustee has a responsibility to protect the trust property from harm, including harm perpetrated by trust beneficiaries.

4) The commons do not belong to the state but belong to commoners, the public.

5) Some commons are the common heritage of all humans and other living beings. Common heritage establishes the right of commoners to those places and goods in perpetuity. This right may not be alienated, denied, repudiated or given away. The Common Heritage law is a limit on one government's sovereignty to claim economic jurisdiction and to exclude some commoners from their share.

6) The precautionary principle is the most useful tool for protecting the commons for this and future generations.

7) Eminent domain is the legal process for moving private property into the commons and shall be used exclusively for that purpose.

8) Infrastructure necessary for humans and other beings to be fully biological and social creatures will reside within the domain of the commons. The positive benefits (externalities) of the commons shall accrue to all commoners.

9) The commons are the foundation of the economy. Therefore the market, commerce and private property shall not externalize damage or costs onto the commons.

10) Damage to or loss of the commons shall be compensated to all commoners.

It is no secret that we face increasing environmental and social degradation. All indicators suggest that prisons are expanding even as crime rates drop, poor children suffer disproportionately from toxic chemicals, global warming and pollution threaten to make the planet uninhabitable and biodiversity is being shredded and homogenized. The old rules enabled the rich to get richer at the expense of the commons – ostensibly so benefits could "trickle down" to everyone else. There may have been a time when those rules made some kind of sense, but now the world is a different place.

It is time to change course. We can create a political and legal agenda based on equitable sharing – sharing the bounty of the Earth in such a way that we increase the commonwealth and common health for this generation and those to come, give substance to the universal declaration of human rights, and fulfill the promise of America. These ten tenets are a place to start.

Carolyn Raffensperger is the executive director of the Science & Environmental Health Network (SEHN) in Ames, Iowa.

THE BEMIDJI STATEMENT ON SEVENTH GENERATION GUARDIANSHIP

The first mandate .... is to ensure that our decision-making is guided by consideration of the welfare and well being of the seventh generation to come.

*I*ndigenous Peoples have learned over thousands of years to live in harmony with the land and the waters. It is our intent to survive and thrive on this planet for this and many generations to come. This survival depends on a living web of relationships in our communities and lands, among humans, and others. The many Indigenous Peoples and cultures from throughout the world are threatened by the disruption of these relationships.

The exploitation and industrialization of the land and water have altered the relationships that have sustained our Indigenous communities. These changes have accelerated in recent years. We are now experiencing the consequences of these actions with increased cancer and asthma rates, suicides, and reproductive disorders in humans, as well as increased hardships of hunting and of whaling. Places that we hold to be sacred have been repeatedly disturbed and destroyed. In animals and in nature we see changing migratory patterns, diseased fish, climate change, extinction of species, and much more.

Government agencies and others in charge of protecting the relationships between our people, the land, air, and water have repeatedly broken treaties and promises. In doing so, they have failed in their duty to uphold the tribal and the public trust. The many changes in these relationships have been well documented, but science remains inadequate for fully understanding their origins and essence. This scientific uncertainty has been misused to carry out economic, cultural, and political exploitation of the land and resources. Failure to recognize the complexity of these relationships will further impair the future health of our people and function of the environment.

The Bemidji Statement on Seventh Generation Guardianship was released July 6, 2006 during the 14th Protecting Mother Earth Conference, convened by the Indigenous Environmental Network in Bemidji, Minnesota.

We value our culture, knowledge, and skills. They are valuable and irreplaceable assets to all of humanity, and help to safe guard the world. The health and well being of our grandchildren are worth more than all the wealth that can be taken from these lands.

By returning to the collective empowerment and decision making that is part of our history, we are able to envision a future that will restore and protect the inheritance of this, and future generations.

Therefore, we will designate Guardians for the Seventh Generation.

Who guards this web of life that nurtures and sustains us all?

Who watches out for the land, the sky, the fire, and the water?

Who watches out for our relatives that swim, fly, walk, or crawl?

Who watches out for the plants that are rooted in our Mother Earth?

Who watches out for the life-giving spirits that reside in the underworld?

Who tends the languages of the people and the land?

Who tends the children and the families?

Who tends the peacekeepers in our communities?

We tend the relationships.

We work to prevent harm.

We create the conditions for health and wholeness.

We teach the culture and we tell the stories.

We have the sacred right and obligation to protect the common wealth of our lands and the common health of our people and all our relations for this generation and seven generations to come. We are the Guardians for the Seventh Generation.

ᏍᎣ

As guardians of the wards over which they were appointed, the manitous [spirits] could withhold from hunters permission or opportunity to kill."

– Basil Johnston, *The Manitous: The Spiritual World of the Ojibway*

ENDNOTES

i   Christopher Shaw, *Sacred Monkey River: A Canoe Trip with the Gods*, W. W. Norton, New York, 2000, p. 140

ii   Robert Sitler, "The Mayan Road."

iii   Christopher Shaw, op. cit. , p. 53

iv   Michael Ortiz Hill, *Dreaming the End of the World: Apocalypse as a Rite of Passage*, Spring Publications, 1994, p. xvi

v   ibid, p. 161

vi   "The Ecologist", 22/09/2001, http://www.ecoglobe.ch/motivation/e/clim2922.htm

vii   Deena Metzger, *Entering the Ghost River: Meditations on the Theory and Practice of Healing*, Hand to Hand, Topanga, CA, 2002, p. 5.

viii   Alan Ereira, *The Elder Brothers*, Alfred A. Knopf, New York, 1992

ix   Metzger, *Entering the Ghost River*, p. 32

x   Alan Ereira, op. cit., p. 1

xi   ibid. p. 228

xii   *The Vision Quest Tarot*, AGM AGMüller. Neuhausen, Switzerland, 1998, pp. 35-36.

xiii   Rachel Pollock, *The Haindl Tarot*, The Minor Arcana, Career Press, Franklin Lakes, NJ, 2002, p. 189

xiv   *The Vision Quest Tarot*, op. cit., p. 83.

xv   Ralph Blum, *The Book of Runes*, St. Martin's Press, New York, 1982

xvi   op cit., Alan Ereria, p. 66

xvii   Stephen Karcher, *Total I Ching, Myths for Change*, TimeWarner Books, UK, 2003, p. 319

xviii   ibid, p. 362.

xix   "Four of Stones, The Power of the Earth," from Rachel Pollack *The Haindl Tarot, The Minor Arcana*, New Page Books, Franklin Lakes, NJ, pp. 135-138.

xx   Karcher, *The Total I Ching*, p. 330

xxi   Metzger, *Entering the Ghost River*, pp. 180-185.

xxii   *Popol Vuh*, translated by Dennis Tedlock, Touchstone, NY, 1996, p. 10.

xxiii   David Freidel, Linda Schele, Joy Parker, *Maya Cosmos*, William Morrow, New York, p. 34.

xxiv   Robert Sitler, "Through Ladino Eyes: Images of the Maya in the Spanish American Novel," 1994.

[xxv]   Joanna Macy, *Widening Circles*, New Society Publishers, Gabriola Island, BC, Canada, 2000. p. 264.

[xxvi]   ibid, pp. 262- 263

[xxvii]   Christoper Shaw, op. cit., p. 313

[xxviii]   Barbara Gowdy, *The White Bone: A Novel*, Picador USA, NY, 1998

[xxix]   "Making It Happen" (IC#28), Quarterly, Spring 1991, p. 20, 1991, 1996 by Context Institute.

[xxx]   *Reno Gazette Journal,* May 10, 2006.

[xxxi]   Karcher, *The Total I Ching*, Hexagram 26, p. 224.

[xxxii]   Richard Seidman, *The Oracle of Kabbalah, Mystical Teachings of the Hebrew Letters*, St. Martin's Press, NY, 2001.

[xxxiii]   Metzger, *Entering the Ghost River*, p. 299.

[xxxiv]   Ibid, p. 304.

[xxxv]   Barbara Tedlock, *The Woman in the Shaman's Body*, Bantam Dell, Random House, NY, 2005, p. 23.

[xxxvi]   *The Vision Quest Tarot*, AGM AGMüller. Neuhausen, Switzerland, 1998, p. 25.

[xxxvii]   Alan Ereira, *The Elder Brothers*, Alfred A. Knopf, 1992

ABOUT THE AUTHOR

Deena Metzger is a novelist, poet, essayist, storyteller and healer. Story is her Medicine. She and her husband Michael Ortiz Hill have brought the tradition of Daré to North America for the sake of restoring beauty and bringing healing to individuals, community and the natural world. Deena is the author of many works including *Entering the Ghost River: Meditations on the Theory and Practice of Healing*, *Tree: Essays and Pieces* and *Writing For Your Life: A Guide and Companion to the Inner Worlds*. She co-edited *Intimate Nature: The Bond Between Women and Animals*. Her novels include *The Other Hand, What Dinah Thought* and *Doors: A Fiction for Jazz Horn*. Her most recent books of poetry are *Looking for the Faces of God* and *A Sabbath Among The Ruins*. Her *New and Selected Poems* is expected to be published in 2008. She is also known for her exuberant "Warrior" poster that illustrates the triumph over breast cancer. She lectures and teaches nationally and internationally, and has developed a training program for the 21st century in the creative, political, spiritual, environmental and ethical aspects of healing. She and her husband live at the end of the road with the wolves Blue, Cherokee and WaYah

The cost of this book reflects the cost of materials and essential labor undertaken by the community around Daré and Hand to Hand. We would greatly appreciate contributions to support the publication and distribution of this book. Make tax-deductible donations to Mandlovu-Hand to Hand c/o International Humanities Center, P.O. Box 923, Malibu, CA 90265, USA. Tel: (310) 579-2069. Or visit Mandlovu online to make a donation at: http://www.ihcenter.org/groups/mandlovu.html. As this book arises from and desires to meet the great need of these times, it is our hope that you will join us in all ways you can in our labor to bring the book to the community and to those who will be informed and sustained by it. Please tell your friends and your colleagues.

Hand to Hand is a community-based endeavor that supports independently published works and public events, free of the restrictions that arise from commercial and political concerns. It is a forum for artists who are in dynamic and reciprocal relationship with their communities for the sake of peacemaking, restoring culture and the planet. For further information about Hand to Hand and Deena Metzger, her writing and work, please see http://www.deenametzger.com or write to her at deenametzger@deenametzger.com or P.O. Box 186, Topanga, CA, 90290, USA.

FOR ADDITIONAL COPIES OF THIS BOOK:

Please contact Book Clearing House at:
(800) 431-1579
or visit their website at:
http://www.bookch.com
or visit your local independent bookseller.

This book is set in Caslon Book and printed on acid-free, recycled paper using vegetable-based inks.

Entering the Council: The Reader's Page